DIFFERENT
D̶I̶S̶ABILITES

**A COLLECTION OF LETTERS FROM
THOSE WHO LOVE SOMEONE WITH
SPECIAL NEEDS**

Compiled By: Chantelle Turner

Different Abilities

Copyright © 2020 Chantelle Turner

All rights reserved. No portion of this book may be reproduced, stored in a retrieval system, or transmitted in any form or by any means; electronic, mechanical, photocopy, recording, scanning, or other, except for brief quotations in critical reviews or articles, without the prior written permission of the authors.

Editing by Clara Rose
Published by RoseDale Publishing

ISBN: 978-1-7344263-5-9

Dedication

To my daughter Kiara,

The day you were born changed our whole lives!

Emergency C-section, you were taken to the NICU, all the tests and eventually finding out that you had an in-utero stroke just before being born. All of that was hard, scary, and surreal. Daddy and I stayed strong, we were with you all eleven days in the NICU, and I will always be grateful for the day we brought you home.

You, my sweet child, are amazing!

We have had our fair share of ups and downs, but in the end, we are always grateful to have you in our lives. At only 6 years old, you have more love and joy inside you than I can ever hope to possess.

You make me a better person every day and it is because of you that this book and the mission of Stronger Mommy exists.

Different Abilities

You my love, are my light. You bring so much joy into the lives of everyone who meets you.

I have no doubt that more hard days will come but I also know that the light will always shine again. You have never let anything hold you back and I will always be here to support you, fight for you, love you, and learn from you.

You are my everything!

Love with all my heart,

Mommy

Chantelle Turner

Acknowledgement

Compiling a book of letters was harder than I thought, and so much more rewarding than I ever could have imagined. I can't count the number of times I cried (happy and sad tears) as I read through each letter.

None of this would have been possible without my family, friends, and Stronger Mommies. While so many people have played a vital role in my life and in this book, I must first start with my husband Eric.

Eric has been my rock, partner, and friend, but most of all, he has been an incredible dad to our daughter Kiara, who inspired this book and the Stronger Mommy Movement. Eric has always supported my dreams, goals, and visions, and he has believed in me, even when I did not always believe in myself. Thank you for your unending support and love.

To Clara Rose who went above and beyond to make sure this book and these incredible letters would be published for the world to read. She worked tirelessly to edit each letter, format the entire book, coach me through the process, and officially publish this incredible book. Without Clara, you would not be reading this book now. Thank you, Clara, for all your hard work.

To Angie Davis Corbett who helped keep this project moving forward by getting more letters, compiling the list of authors, and overall keep me on track and motivated throughout this project. Thank you for making sure these incredible letters made their way into this book.

Different Abilities

Finally, a huge thank you goes out to all the Stronger Mommies who took the time to submit their incredible letters. This book is just a small sample of all the incredible Stronger Mommies out there, and I know by sharing your letters with the world, you are making a positive impact on everyone who reads them.

Table of Contents

Dedication 3

Acknowledgement 5

Preface 9

To My Younger Self 15

To My Daughter 37

To My Partner 69

To My Son 79

To Those Outside 111

To Someone Who Needs to Hear it 123

To a Doctor 143

To the Person Who Made a Difference 155

From Family 163

Contributors 181

About Chantelle Turner 186

Different Abilities

Preface

> "To the world you may be one person, but to me you are the world."
>
> – Brandi Snyder

Dear Reader,

When my daughter was born, I had no idea I would someday dream of changing the world for her. At the time I lived moment to moment, solely focused on getting her everything I could, so she could have the best possible life. It is what I think all mothers want for their children really. I set out to find her what she needed. I was an island and that was perfectly ok with me.

My friends all had nuro-typical children and thought I was some-kind of super mom (I am not). I spent the first few years of my daughter's life not really knowing any other families that had children with special needs, and that was ok.

For the most part, we were happy. I got what she needed, I found and fought for the resources, and I saw my daughter thrive because of it.

Different Abilities

Eventually, I ventured into the online support communities designed for parents that had children with special needs. There I discovered that somehow; me with my degree in Theatre Arts, just one single child, and zero formal training... somehow had the answers to most of their questions.

I found so few parents knew about all the services, support, resources, and communities at their disposal. Most of all, I realized while there was a LOT out there for our kids, there really was nothing for us as the parents.

Almost by accident, Stronger Mommy was born. Founded with the intent to focus on helping other special needs parents just like me, get the resources, services, support, and community we need, so we could be the best possible parents for our kids!

For the past year and half, and hopefully for many years to come, I have served this community with all my heart. I have made it my mission to help these parents and their amazing kids with different abilities. Somewhere along the road, I came to serve you as well. This book, and these letters, were written just for you. It was designed to help those on the outside to better understand this special-needs chaos that many of us live in. To give you just a little insight into a world that looks much different than you probably imagine.

It is not your fault, you do not get it, heck, I did not get it before I lived it. Read these letters. Laugh with us, cry with us, and better understand us. Smile when you see us and our kids. I truly believe that understanding is the key to a better world.

To my fellow special-needs parents, this book is for you as well. As you read these letters you may feel the echo of your own story within them. I hope as you read them, you realize you are not alone.

While all our journeys are different, each one of us and our amazing kids, leave a lasting impression upon this world. I hope the letters here inspire you to write one of your own. Someone special in your life, or maybe even a stranger, needs to read it.

Finally, for the amazing children and adults with DIFFERENT abilities, this book and its letters are especially for you! No matter how many hard days there are, you are so deeply loved. For all the words you may not be able to speak or the hugs your body does not like to give, we cherish you.

When times are hard, when you struggle, and even when we seem mad, frustrated, or upset, we are grateful for you. YOU light up our lives and fill us with purpose, not in spite-of your differences but BECAUSE of them! Never be ashamed of who you are. Never focus on the things you cannot do. Your life and your potential are limitless.

Believe in yourself and anything is possible!

Chantelle Paige Turner

Different Abilities

Chantelle Turner

Different Abilities

Chapter One
To My Younger Self

"Life can only be understood backwards: but it must be lived forwards."

– Soren Kierkegaard

Dear 23-year-old Angie,

It may sound strange, saying hi to my younger self, but I know how bad you were hurting that day. I want you to know, although you tried to be brave and hide behind a strong mask for the sake of your family, your feelings at 23 years old made a huge impact on your future.

I am much older now, but I can feel those emotions in the blink of an eye. I wish the person and mother I have become, could have been there with you, to help ease your fears. Instead, I am writing a backwards time capsule letter to you. Although I was not there with you then, pieces of you are here with me now, and I want to reach into that part of myself and help you.

August 9th, 2003, your baby boy Dominik was diagnosed with brutonsagamma-globulinanemia X linked with neutropenia. (Brutons for short.) I remember vividly the fear you felt, the helplessness you felt; but most importantly, the soul crushing guilt you experienced.

You were a new mother, proud in every way of the ten fingers and ten toes on his seemingly perfect body, but you instinctually knew something wasn't quite right. You sat with your son in your arms, holding him tightly, rocking him, running your fingers through his hair, while the sound of machines beeped in a sterile cold hospital.

His tiny body was hooked up to his first-of many-infusions and you kept saying softly to him, "Mommy is so sorry, Mommy is so, so, sorry." You stroked his cheek as tears streamed down your own, begging him in your mind and heart to forgive you.

We were immediately admitted to the hospital, straight from the doctor's office. It was a whirlwind nightmare, with Doctors not being able to answer questions, to the nurse not securing the IV, and my hysterical 10-month-old ripping the IV out, which then required a special team. It took five of us to hold him down so they could get a good IV access. In the middle of all this, we were told the illness was genetic, passed from mother to son... I had made my son sick. Words no parent wants to hear.

At 23, I'm not sure how or where you pulled the strength from to challenge the doctors, to know what questions to ask, when you couldn't even begin to process what was happening!

Every time you were faced with another symptom or met another doctor, the same guilty thought played like a record in your mind, "Sweet baby boy, please forgive me."

You could barely breathe when you tried to imagine explaining to Dom why or how he had been given this cruel genetic fate. But you kept moving, you kept pushing forward.

Once Dominik was released from the hospital, you and your husband were sent to a genetic counselor. It was then you discovered, for sure, which parent was the carrier of this hideous gene, and if you were ever to have any more children: girls would be the carrier and boys would have the illness.

So, now there was no denying it. All the guilt you had been beating yourself up with now was confirmed; the results of the test now deepened the bruises of self-blame and punishment.

Now you felt a sadness beyond Dominik's disease. You felt the reality of your situation and understood Dominik would not only be fighting for his health, but he would do it as an only child; without a little sister or brother to tease and depend upon. The life you imagined for yourself (since high school) changed in that moment forever.

The next few years were spent falling deeper into that black hole of blame and taking every precaution to keep Dom away from any germs or potential for germs. You read every book and article you could get your hands on about your son's illness and how to keep him safe.

You learned Brutons is a very rare auto-immune disorder. Essentially meaning Dominik doesn't have a functioning immune system. Your life would soon turn into constant doctor visits, IV infusions, and complete isolation.

Being in your early twenties, you were scared, you were the mom that allowed the diagnosis to take over. You missed moments with your son. You were physically there, but mentally you were scanning the room, the people, worrying every moment that he would get sick.

Being a mom in a constant state of panic was not only unfair to yourself, but most importantly to your son. The old mantra of "forgive me" still rang in your ears every day. You felt that you needed to be punished on some level.

Your biggest dream was to be a mother, this was going to be a challenge. The doctors had advised against pregnancy, not because you had any knowledge of this awful gene, but for your own safety.

You had been diagnosed with multiple female issues, and after you married your high school sweetheart, you had 4 angel babies before being blessed with your beautiful son.

You went through a lot of pain and loss before you were rewarded with the love of your life: Dominik. Despite everything that had happened (and could still happen,) October 3rd, 2002 would always remain the best day of your life.

Eventually, with a lot of counseling, family support, and soul searching you became the advocate your son needed. You became a strong woman, you became a confident woman, you became the mom Dom needed.

You allowed yourself to begin to live in the moment. You allowed yourself to listen to the joy of Dom's belly laughs. You studied his face, relaxed yourself, and let the feeling of being on high alert still be there but more on the sideline.

You questioned your place in life and your dream of becoming a prosecutor went out the window, but you allowed yourself to feel the honor of being his mom.

Even when each new diagnosis came in you became the world's best researcher, you knew he was on the spectrum before the doctors did, you got him in to see all the right specialists to get him the right help. You were your son's advocate.

You, my young strong woman became so much more than just a mom, you became a nurse, care giver, meds dispenser, fixer of all things, his comfort, and at times his punching bag for the anger that grew.

He was becoming older and more aware he wasn't like other

Different Abilities

kids. You went through a divorce and you've had to make some tough decisions on your own. You had no idea how strong and capable you were and still to this day are.

I can't even count how many sleepless nights you've had, but always got up and done what was needed. Doctors, infusions, counseling for both of you and much more.

I want you to know that despite all your guilt and constant *I'm Sorry,* through that year and beyond, your baby boy did not hate you for his illness. In fact, he loved you more for being the mom that didn't give up. He called you his "warrior mom," because through every fever and pain of his childhood, you fought alongside him and didn't give up.

I want you to know it hasn't been easy and it will take you every second of 16 years, to feel you deserve a title such as WARRIOR, but now it is proudly tattooed on your arm. The mask of strength you used to wear isn't as fake as it was then. Now, you have battle scars and war paint across your cheeks, and you are much more confident.

Today, you are 39 years old and it's still not easy. Every day I have a moment where I beg God for Dominik to be healthy. We have a different normal than the conventional definition of the word, and that's OK. It's our normal, and to be honest, our normal is beautiful and full of love. I wish I had this mindset at your age, but I guess that's why they call it a journey.

So, strong 23-year-old self, I am so proud of you, the

struggles haven't hardened you. You are a good mother, you are knowledgeable, you are confident, and you don't back down when it comes to your gut instinct, you are Dom's champion.

Now you've learned how to handle the many struggles and crossed over many hurdles that have come our way. You did it! You have gotten Dom through every single one. You are Dom's warrior!

Now, I do still have my moments. I think back to that night, at 2am, tears flowing, and begging my son to forgive me, but I know that it is a piece in time and not the hopeless ending it seemed. It's good to go back there on occasion, to see how far we have come together as mother and son.

In our beautiful normal, I've learned humility, what it means to be humble, and the gut grabbing definition of true love. We have been blessed with life-long friends that are more like family now. Most importantly, I've learned acceptance.

So, to summarize for you, my younger self, you and Dom become warriors and experts in every diagnosis.

Oh, and Angie... to answer the question you kept asking yourself that night, "Will I ever laugh again?" Oh sweetheart, you do! You laugh often and loud.

You wondered if you would ever smile again, you smile more times a day than you can count! You have an amazing support team. I know you were so worried you'd never smile again. The initial pain was so deep, too raw, too sharp. You

Different Abilities

do Angie, even if the tears are flowing because you got dealt yet another blow, you smile!

I don't know where we would be without our infusion angels: Denise, Becky, Amber, Lori, Nichole, and Genie. We wouldn't be where we are now, that's for sure.

A parting piece of advice for moms just receiving their child's diagnosis. Remember to just keep swimming, we use that a lot! (Finding nemo was a source of comfort for Dom during treatment.)

It's going to feel like you can't breathe, let alone figure your way through this, but look at your child, see them smiling? Hear them laughing? That is your motivation. You'll be your own champion of your own beautiful normal! You got this momma!

So, 23-year-old self, I want to thank you. For all your worry and fear... maybe it felt lonely and painful, and I'm sorry for that, but you grew from it! You became a better person for yourself, your friends, your family, and your son.

You no longer need a mask to hide behind; you share your strength with others, so they don't feel so lost and lonely. The desire to be forgiven is replaced now with gratitude for all the moments you've been granted with your son.

Thank you, it is due to the choices you made in your 23rd year that made the difference. Thank you for never giving up... no matter what came your way. You are the reason I am the warrior mom today.

With love, your current 39-year-old self,

Angie

Different Abilities

Dear Younger Self,

(You know... before I had kids and I knew everything.)

You don't know it yet, but three of your four children will have very demanding health challenges. You'll commonly refer to them as Special-Needs children.

I'm sure this will come as a complete surprise to you since, right now you have no inkling or feeling that this will happen. You expect that just like everyone else in your family, you will have perfectly healthy children, with no need for extra visits to the doctor, other than their yearly check-ups.

It will not be easy, but it will be feasible. It will not be a walk in the park. It will be a really difficult walk, actually, think of walking up a big steep hill in a park, while it's raining... no pouring... no snowing, and you are rock climbing... yea that's more like it. But know this... you will have support all around you, and you aren't in this adventure alone.

Now let me tell you how incredible your children will be.

Your oldest will have 6 surgeries before he is 1 year old, and he will have 15 surgeries by the time he's in the fourth grade.

But he will also get 3rd place in the Science Bee at school. When you pick him up from school, five different kids will call him by name and wave bye to him.

Every teacher you sit down with in parent-teacher

conference, will tell you how much they LOVE having him in their class. He will get straight A's and he'll get his homework done during the 15 minutes-drive home from school.

He will read huge novels on a regular basis, practice the piano on his own, and you'll be able to count on one hand how many times you've seen him fight with one of his siblings.

You will have another son, who will get very sick when he is 1 year old. It will be a tough ride, full of surgeries and an exploratory endoscopy to see what is making him so sick. No doctors ever figure out why he is on the brink of death for a year and a half. But don't worry.

When he is 2 1/2 years-old, after another night in the ER with him, you will fall asleep on your mother-in-law's couch and have a dream. In that dream, someone will come to you and tell you exactly what is making your son so sick. When you wake up, you change his diet and he'll never be sick again, just as long as he keeps to his strict diet.

He is loving and will volunteer to help you almost every day. He will learn to work hard and even learns how to cook his own food and pack his own lunch, by the time he is in the first grade.

Your little girl, who is not special needs, will have her own challenges as every child does, but since she is surrounded by brothers with special needs, she grows up being very needed. Because of that, she learns to serve with her whole

Different Abilities

heart, and she loves being your buddy, your helper, and your friend.

The next son you have will be very special. He will cause you the most stress and the most sorrow, the most joy and appreciation for life.

He will be diagnosed with Autism Spectrum Disorder and Apraxia of Speech. He will be non-verbal. He will wake up in the night and hurt himself by banging his head repetitively against the wall. He will be over stimulated visually and will clear everything off every surface in the house. He will knock down every piece of furniture he can get his hands on, so you will learn to decorate differently!

He will need constant care and will learn about 100 times slower than a typical child. But he will learn, and every hour of therapy that you drive him to, and every song you sing to him and play for him, and every book you read to him will make a difference.

He will connect with you and he will know that you are his mother. One night when it is dark and quiet, he will walk right up to you and look you in the eye and point to you and say "Mama." He only does this once, but it will be a gift you'll hold on to the rest of your life.

You will love this son with a love so deep, so strong, you don't even know that this kind of love exists until you have him. He will be close to heaven but will bring Heaven and Hell to your home. He will be your spiritual compass and you wouldn't trade him for the world.

Remember young-self, I know right now, you and your college roommates are kinda boy-crazy. You are obsessed with your dates, dances, finals, and new outfits. That is fine for now, but not important. Your children will make you grow up. And when you grow up, you'll be glad you did.

This life isn't about what you check off your *To Do list*. It's about who you become in the process. Life is a time to prepare yourself to be the kind person that will be comfortable in the presence of your maker.

And your children help you do that more than anything else in your life.

Love, Your future self.

Different Abilities

To Myself,

I know you've always hated to be yourself. Perhaps it's because people often make fun of you. As far back as I can remember, you've been trying to change yourself, just to be acceptable to others. *Others,* who don't value your strengths or your positivity. Others who don't have anything to do with your life.

You kept losing faith in yourself, feeling like a failure at every step of life, so you figured life was just meaningless. Until one day, when you decided to stand up for yourself.

It was the day you first saw your life partner. He was a simple guy, with a beautiful mind. He brought you lots of hope and possibilities in life. In his eyes, you saw life. You shared the same feelings, thoughts, and ideas.

You fought for him and you got him. You knew from that day on you would have someone in your life who was worth fighting for. You knew it was LOVE. The best part was you never had to look back. You kept moving forward.

Just when you thought you had enough on your plate, autism came into your life. You wanted a little more time to settle down, but now you had a child that would require therapy. You thought therapy would be a cure, you were mistaken.

You decided you would have to forget about resting or taking breaks in life. No mommy time, you'd need to shift gears and live a different life than you had expected. You ran around, aimlessly and endlessly.

You work hard every day, but without a paycheck. You visit friends, hoping for some time to just gossip a bit, but you are constantly reminded, "Hey, don't forget the autism!"

You wish someone would come forward and say, "It's okay, take a break and I'll watch the kids." Mostly they don't. Even if they do, you know they are not sincere, and it makes you sick to your stomach.

A new fear is added to your life, your fear of leaving your child alone in this wild world.

Please, don't stress yourself so much. Take a break and some deep breaths. Let a moment of silence take you back to a when you spent some time with your dear brother. He was always there for you no matter what. You could create an entire book from those memories, use them for strength.

Then come back to your life. Tomorrow is another day and you will keep fighting.

Yours faithfully,

Me

Different Abilities

Dear Stephanie,

No one told you that when you met the love of your life, you would be expecting a miracle baby shortly after.

I'm here to let you know that it's ok. It's okay to laugh. It's okay cry. It's okay not to be okay.

The journey you are about to go through is an amazing journey of patience, love, and faith. The journey started November 2016, when you found out you were pregnant.

You told only your fiancé. He was so overjoyed because he had wanted children for so long! Then you told your mother in law. She was super happy for the both of you. Then your parents and sister, your mom said she'd always be there for you!

The pregnancy progressed, you had the regular morning sickness and had to run to the bathroom to go pee every ten minutes!

Everything was good until month five, when everything became a fast-paced run. You learned the baby was a boy, but the OB was concerned at not seeing your son's stomach. You panicked, if he doesn't have a stomach, he won't be able to eat!

You'll be sent off to a specialist in Springfield IL where the specialist will confirm he has a stomach! But he has a mass where his lung should be. They will send you to another specialist who is better equipped to handle your situation.

When see the next specialist, he tells you that it's the biggest mass he's seen, and he's only done four surgeries, similar to the one your son will need. You'll be given five options.

You must make a decision that day because your options are limited, you'll choose life! You choose to start off with steroids and you will get two rounds, two shots each time. It'll hurt but you won't mind if it'll help your son.

Within a week of getting your first round, the specialist says that he notices the mass shrinking! Praise Jesus!! The mass is shrinking, it is a good sign because it means less stress on your son!

With everything going well, the OB says you will deliver down in St. Louis. Your son won't have surgery to remove the mass until at least six months to a year after he's born!! You will be induced July 2, 2017 and deliver July 3, 2017! Except, that didn't go to plan.

One rainy night in May 2017, the thunder went boom and your water broke. You thought you'd peed yourself. So, you go clean up and lay down for a bit and notice that you start having cramps.

With this being your first pregnancy, you don't think much of it and don't say anything to your fiancé. Thirty minutes later you feel a lot of pressure and finally tell him. He gets you to the car and you drive to Springfield IL where they know your case.

The doctor says that you are 5cm dilated and that he can't

Different Abilities

stop your son from coming. They hook you up to things and get the show on the road. When they start to lose both your heart rates, they will take you to the operating room. You thought there was still time for Lamaze class, so you just ask them what you should do.

Your son arrives and goes up to the NICU and they work on you for a little bit. About an hour later you will be allowed to see your son.

You can't hold him just yet. But you know he's alive. So, you talk to him and hum to him, and finally go back to your room to sleep. You pray to God that he keeps your little boy alive because you don't want to feel that heartache.

Two days pass and the doctor will say he's stable enough to fly by helicopter to St. Louis where they can give him better care.

You say see you later to your little one and go home to check on the cats and get clothes for your stay. Let's be honest, you don't know how long you'll be there.

When you get to the hospital and get settled, you have an opportunity to get a room at the McDonald house, it's a small room but that's okay because you need sleep.

Time will pass and you will take your son home. Your fiancé will get an unexpected appendectomy. Things happen.

Your son will go in for his first surgery at 25 days old. He'll get pneumonia in the cyst, in the mass, and antibiotics couldn't get rid of it, so surgery will have to. The surgery only takes two hours! That scares you and your fiancé but he's doing well.

The next day though the docs are worried about his CO_2 output. It's not great, so they put him on nitrate oxide. This helps tremendously!

Months pass and they will start weaning him off his oxygen and sedation meds. By August of 2017, he's on CPAP of 10! Blessings!!

Perhaps because of the stress, you have been eating too many sweets and end up having gallbladder surgery. That's ok.

Your son goes in for another surgery to get a g-tube. He won't know how to properly do the suck, swallow, and breathe technique. He comes out of it ok but is intubated for a week following the surgery.

After that he's extubated, he returns to CPAP of 10. He's on it for a while before they wean him down to CPAP of 6. Then finally they get him down to 0.5 liters and he can go home!!!

December 27th, 2017 you finally go home. You will be home for ten days then head back to the NICU. The Doctors are puzzles at first, but winter is hard on those babies. You get released but are back within two weeks.

Next, your apartment will get flooded and you need to move in with your mother-in-law. That's ok.

Different Abilities

Your son will be in and out of the hospital until May 2018. That's okay. During the February hospital stay, he gets a GJ tube. He's now getting fed through his intestines. He isn't throwing up anymore!! That's wonderful!

For the next year he's home. No hospital visits, no nothing!!

In March 2019, he will have eye surgery. You have never experienced him without sedation and waking up from anesthesia. It's awful. His oxygen keeps going down, you will panic. Now your husband will panic. You stay for three days.

For the next week, your son will mostly sleep, trying to recover from it. But both his eyes focus, at the same time!! It's wonderful!

From then on, it'll be only appointments and therapy for him to learn how to walk. Some days it'll be hard. But mostly it'll be rewarding! Just to see him meet all those milestones!

Yes, you will be jealous of those other babies and toddlers who can walk, talk, crawl, and sit by themselves. That's ok. Your son will meet those milestones in his own time. You need to be patient.

Words of wisdom: what you go through may seem like the worst thing in the world, but if you have family alongside you, you will be okay.

Your future self, Stephanie

Different Abilities

Chapter Two

To My Daughter

"Very little is needed to make a happy life; it is all within yourself, in your way of thinking."

– Marcus Aurelius

My name is Cloresa, I am a single mom to twins. My letter is to Avery my twin A.

Dear Avery,

You were my blessing before you were my miracle. I wasn't supposed to have any more babies, especially not twins. Shock turned to joy, then turned to overwhelming love.

This road, like all of life's roads, did not promise to be bump free, and we hit our share of potholes.

At fifteen weeks your water sac broke, and I was told I would lose my babies. I went home to mourn and went to my doctors appt two weeks later, expecting to hear of my loss.

There were no words for my joy at hearing her say, "I

thought you said her water broke." I had to show my doctor the ultrasound from the ER visit to prove it. Your sac had resealed and refilled, it was a miracle they said.

We knew the newly repaired sac was weak, and another break would happen, but I didn't expect it so soon. At twenty-six weeks, we were back at the hospital this time to stay. They wanted me to make it to thirty-four weeks to give sister a chance, but they were concerned I might get an infection from you.

The doctors said you would pass in a few days, this time your sac hadn't just broke, it had ruptured like a burst balloon and the pieces were wrapped around, so you couldn't move anything but your legs. You had nothing holding the fluid around your head or face, which would allow you to breath, or swallow it.

I cried and I prayed. You fought. Your pulse stayed strong in the 140's but they told me I would only have a couple hours with you, if you made it through your birth. At thirty-one weeks and 6 days, the contractions started.

It was bittersweet, I wanted to see your beautiful faces, but I wasn't ready to say goodbye to you. I had to have an emergency spinal for the c-section, and then everything went so fast. You came first but I didn't get to see your face. You didn't cry. They balled you up in a sheet and walked out with you. It was hard not to cry while they delivered your sister.

I didn't recover from the spinal for seven hours and then was taken to my room. I asked to see you both, I wanted to see you even though I knew it was too late.

The nurse thought I had already been to the NICU, so when I told her I had not, she went right out for a wheelchair. They took me to the sickest baby part of the NICU, and there was Arwyn, so tiny at only 3.8lbs. I couldn't touch her she was still so fragile.

Then the nurse says, "And here's sister." There you were, 2.13lbs, with blue lights and tubes in your mouth and nose. The machine was forcing breaths into you that shook your whole body, but you fought.

You couldn't swallow, since you didn't have amniotic fluid to swallow for so long, those muscles didn't work. You couldn't move anything but your legs, you had not been able to move for so long, your body was stiff, and the muscles gone. But you were beautiful, and you fought.

They gave you a g-tube at 2 months, saying it wouldn't work because you were too sick, but you fought. When you gained 8lbs in two weeks, they had to reduce your calories and feeding rate.

We were sent to Dallas for answers. They gave you a trach to protect your airway, because you couldn't swallow and had preemie reflux. You aspirated the reflux fluid and almost died, so the trach was inserted to help suction safely.

Two days after the trach was inserted, you developed NEC. It

Different Abilities

attacked your intestines, they had to remove 60% of your intestines. They asked me to remove you from life support, explaining that the human body literally cannot survive with that much intestine gone, and intestine transplants on babies don't take. I couldn't do it, I had promised to fight for as long as you fought, and you fought.

They gave you Morphine and Versed and told me to have family come say goodbye, you wouldn't make it thru the night. I sat and counted each breath until I fell asleep, but you fought.

A few weeks later, as they decided it was time to attempt a reconnection of the intestines, they told me it wouldn't work. You would need a colostomy bag, since all your intestine was basically gone and wouldn't reach.

The maximum time allowed for babies to be under anesthesia in Texas is four hours, they would try. The surgery was done in an hour. The reconnection was perfect and with only a teaspoon of blood lost.

We have been told you would be a vegetable at 7 months old, I laugh when I remember that, watching you roll around the crib now at two years old trying to grab at things outside the crib.

My blessing, My miracle, My fighter.

I love you so, Mama

To my daughter Antoinette,

I knew. I knew there was something different when you were an infant and never cried. People said you were a good baby, but I sensed it. When I would say your name, you would search around the room to focus on anything, but me. I admit, I thought, *Well, she's just not interested in mommy.*

I would sit with you, but you would just *ignore* me. Even when you were mobile, you would play around the whole room without ever once interacting with me. I often wished I was a character in your favorite show. I mastered Elmo's voice in anticipation of grabbing your attention and it worked, for a few seconds.

Some parents can't get their kids to leave their beds, but I wanted you to feel comfort and cuddle so much, that I tried to pull you in.

You never looked at me, and I knew. When I told Daddy what I felt, he was in denial. You see, when you were born prematurely, it destroyed us. That was the hardest thing we have ever been through, but this was going to top it.

How could somebody so precious go through so much in their life, it wasn't fair. We felt the more we celebrated your delayed milestones, the less real the other things would be.

When we saw other people posting on Facebook about the accomplishments of the much younger children, it began to sink in. Oh, so painfully it sunk in.

Different Abilities

Every day it became more and more obvious something was wrong. When you turned two, we finally had the assessment done. We had a diagnosis. **Autism.**

Even though I knew, I didn't know what that would feel like. Nothing had changed, yet everything had.

It felt surreal to tell others that I'm an autism Mom. I thought, *Maybe I shouldn't say it, because maybe it will change.* But it didn't. This was our life now. I'm not sad at all. I'm actually thankful that God picked Daddy and me to love you!

Even though I'm not sad, I grieve. I grieve for the life I thought you would have. I grieve, because I feel you've already been dealt more than any person should have. I worry about my age and how I will die at some point, leaving you. I feel guilt that school was so easy for me, but you will face the hardship I never had to.

I have a promise though. No matter what, I will never give up on you. Daddy and I will never stop being your advocates. You are our hero. People may not even know this, but there are two stages of our lives... before Autism and after.

In the after, Mommy is going to try and change the world.

You, my love, are my inspiration.

Love always, Mommy

My Dearest Savanna,

The day I found out I was pregnant with you I was so happy. My pregnancy was great.

The day you were born I knew there was something wrong. You would turn blue when you ate. You would pause in your breathing longer than you should. You would not gain weight. It was almost two years before we finally had answers.

You have been through so many surgeries and procedures in your first five years of life. There are days I wish I could take it all from you.

Now you are about to graduate preschool. You are a happy 5 year old, you smile through everything, and I know you're going to do great things when you grow up.

Love You,

Mommy

Different Abilities

Olivia,

The day I found out I was pregnant with you my whole life changed for the better.

Just 5 short months into being pregnant, they told me that you had down syndrome, my heart was shattered.

Mommy didn't know anything about down syndrome at that time, so I prepared myself for the worst, as the doctors told me you probably wouldn't make it to one year old.

You were born December 8th, 2010 at 7 lbs. 12 oz. I knew the minute I heard your cry you were going to be a fighter. You were able to come home with me two days later.

When you were 6 months old you had open heart surgery. My fear came true, as the nurse came in the waiting room and told me that they were trying everything they could to revive you. I was in shock, I didn't know what to say, what to do, or how to feel.

A short time later she came back and said that you were stable, and they just finished closing you up and cleaning you.

A couple hours later, I was allowed to see you. You had the cutest little bow in your hair and looked like a little angel. They said it would be a bumpy road, but you were a fighter.

As I held your little hand, you gripped my finger and gave me a little smile. I knew right then you would be okay. Just ten short days later you came home.

Chantelle Turner

You are now eight years old and the absolute light of my life. You have shown me what it's like to fight and never give up!

You are and always will be, my hero!

I love you buggy

Love,

Mommy

Different Abilities

To my beautiful daughter,

I wanted you before I ever knew I was going to have you. I prayed for you. From the moment I found out I was pregnant I loved you with everything I had.

After my first doctor's appointment they called me to ask me to come back the next day. My heart sank when they told me something wasn't right. My hormone level was 1% away from the point when you miscarry.

My doctor told me she would do everything she could but that there was a chance I would lose you. I knew I would do whatever it took to keep you, because even though I had just found out about you, I already couldn't imagine my life without you.

I did everything the doctor said and trust me it wasn't easy. I got so many pokes. I had to have my blood drawn three times a week to check my hormone levels, and I had to take hormone replacement pills to bring my level up for you.

I also had to have an ultrasound once a week to check on how you were doing. It was my favorite part of my week, I got to see my sweet girl.

Just when everything started to go well and we didn't have to see the doctor as much, I fell and hurt my hip.

I had to go on bedrest for the rest of my pregnancy. I scheduled a C-section to be your birthday, the day I would finally meet my sweet baby girl.

When I held you in my arms, I couldn't believe how perfect you were. I loved you more than I had ever loved.

When you were a couple weeks-old we had to go to children's hospital and have a scope done. It turned out you had laryngomalacia and vocal cord paralysis.

You had a scope every couple of months, until you grew out of the laryngomalacia when you were a year old. You will have the vocal cord paralysis for life but that's okay, so does mommy.

When you were two, I noticed your feet looked different when you walked. I called your doctor freaking out and he sent you to an orthopedic doctor. They told me you just had flat feet and not to worry.

Oh, my sweet girl I should have pushed harder. I'm so sorry I didn't.

We had a normal life, and everything was good. Over the years you would complain about your feet and I would bring it up to the doctor. No one was worried. They told me to buy you better shoes.

I was already buying you name brand shoes and feeling the arch of each one to make sure you had support.

When you turned 6 you really started complaining that they hurt more than before. I bought you two new pair of shoes in one month trying to find something to help relieve your pain.

Different Abilities

One day in the bookstore you sat down in the middle of the floor and took off your shoe to rub your foot. That's when I decided you needed to see a different doctor. I called children's hospital and made you an appointment with an orthopedic specialist.

At first look he said the same thing as everyone else, that you were flat footed. Just when I thought we had another doctor who wasn't going to listen he said, "I want to take some X-rays just as a precaution." Oh, my love, I thank God he listened. I thank God he took those X-Rays; I will be forever grateful to him.

They let me stay in the X-ray room because you were scared, it helped you to have mommy close. As soon as the image showed up on the screen my heart dropped.

Oh, my sweet girl, I can't even begin to understand the pain you have been in all this time. When I saw your bones, I knew something was seriously wrong and our life was about to change.

You were diagnosed with pronation deformity. The bones in your feet didn't form correctly and they aren't straight.

The day you were diagnosed you were so scared, and I was strong for you all day. I held your hand, smiled, and told you it would be ok. That night after you were asleep, I cried like a baby.

I couldn't afford my insurance deductible for the braces that you needed, so you started seeing a specialist in another state who didn't make me pay my deductible.

They diagnosed you with more than we originally thought. You were officially diagnosed with pronation deformity, c foot, decreased body awareness, skew foot, flat feet, low muscle tone in your legs, and one of your hips is starting to turn inward.

Oh, my sweet girl, after that appointment mommy cried so hard. I can't even put into words the way I felt, knowing all these years you were struggling with so much.

We now have physical therapy multiple times a week to help your muscles develop. I know sometimes you think I'm hard on you because you want to play during physical therapy instead of working. But my love I'm not trying to be hard on you, I just want to help you. I want you to get better and to not be in pain.

Right now, you are so confused, you don't understand why this happened to you. My love I wish I knew why, but mommy doesn't know either.

You ask me how long our life will be like this. How long you will have to go to physical therapy. I can't answer that question because mommy just doesn't know how long it is going to take for you to develop your muscles.

You cried when you found out you are going to have to wear your braces for years. I don't have the heart to tell you there is a chance it will be for life.

Different Abilities

Our life has definitely changed in the last couple of months but there are some things I want you to know.

First, I love you with all my heart and soul, please never forget that.

I also want you to know, no matter what, mommy will be by your side the whole time. Remember, we have always been a team and that isn't ever going to change.

I also need you to know that I'm sorry. I am so very sorry that we didn't find out sooner what was going on with you. The guilt I feel for not knowing sooner, eats away at me and I'm trying to forgive myself, so that I can be better for you. Right now, you need me at my best.

I know that you can overcome all your obstacles and I will be next to you holding your hand, cheering you on, pushing you to keep going, whatever you need.

I am blessed to be your mom. I love you so much McKenzi. Together, we've got this, it is the start of our journey.

I love you forever.

Love,

Mom

Evangelein,

My sweet, stubborn, sassy, four-year-old, angel baby. You were diagnosed with DDX3X gene mutation last year. You have a very rare, unique mutation. Which doesn't surprise me because you are so rare and unique.

You can't walk, talk, or understand most things we talk about. But you are the light of my life and my most favorite conversation.

We will likely spend the rest of my life together. You will live with me and I will care for you until the day I die.

I want you to know that people will, and have, said negative things about you. You will struggle, but you will prevail. You will learn to let mean things roll off your back and learn to make life work in your favor.

Raising you these past four years has been full of surgeries, unknowns, I don't know and learning to love the doctors, hospitals, and nurses.

You have been through more than some adults will their whole life. All the while with a smile on your face, a giggle, or a kiss blown to whoever you see. Mostly the boys, my little sassy heartbreaker.

Please continue to teach me, your family, and everyone around you what pure happiness is. What it is to accept anyone and everyone.

Different Abilities

Most of all teach ME what it is to be strong and selfless. To love without boundaries, and to know that it's okay to be scared and make a great comeback.

I definitely need you more than you need me angel girl.

Love,

The strong, sometimes scared, always loving you,

Umm (mom)

Dear Savanna,

The last 5 ½ years has been a roller coaster ride, to say the least.

From the day you were born, I know there was something special about you, and I continue to see just how special you are.

At three days old you were diagnosed with OSA (Obstructive Sleep Apnea) and CSA (Central Sleep Apnea).

At 8 months old, we found out about the hole in your heart, PDA.

At a year in a half old, we found out about your chromosome deletion 18p11.2 microdeletion.

You have been through so much, from heart surgery, to other surgeries, MRI's, hospital stays, and Cat scans. Still you are sweet, bright, and loving!

I can't wait to see what the years to come has for us but know that we are taking it on together.

Love you always,

Mommy

Different Abilities

My Dearest Violet,

When I was a little girl, I dreamed of having a daughter. A daughter with red curls and moss colored eyes, who danced and sang, and who ran around my house, with her little feet going tap-tap-tap in shiny black shoes.

So, when I learned that you were indeed going to be my little girl, finally, after two brothers, I was overjoyed. One of the first things I bought for you was a pair of shiny little black shoes.

Then you were born, you were tiny and perfect. You had the red hair, the moss colored eyes, you were sweet tempered and lovely, and those little black shoes sat on a shelf, waiting for you to wear them. But you never did.

Before you ever had the chance to walk, to run, or to dance, some dark entity reached down and twisted both of your legs. I carried you, six months old, limp as a newborn, into the children's hospital.

The doctors told me your diagnosis and told me solemnly that you would likely never walk. They shook their heads and said they had no idea what your future would look like.

I had never heard the words transverse myelitis before that moment. It had never occurred to me that you would not walk. You were perfect and beautiful, and you looked fine.

It took a few months, and several missed milestones, but the idea that you would never walk settled into my mind, like so many other little facts. My birthday is October twenty-fifth. I live in Utah. Donald Trump is the President. Violet will never walk.

But those little black shoes stayed on the shelf, never worn and mocking me, you thought... you thought!

One night, in a fit of pique, I threw them in the garbage can to silence them. I knelt on the floor and sobbed wretchedly for the both of us. For stolen dreams and a potential never to be realized. I choked on the words, "but I love her, but I love her," as though my love was a spell of protection, I could cloak you in.

Eventually the tears dried up and I got up and moved on with a new little fact in my brain: My birthday is October twenty-fifth. I live in Utah. Donald Trump is the President. Violet will never walk. It doesn't matter. I love Violet.

It got easier. The understanding welled within me, I could, and I did, love my daughter. The child in front of me, even though the image of the child I wanted had been ripped to pieces, imbued me with strength – I could roll with this. I could make life good for you.

You, however, didn't seem to know that you were not supposed to walk. While you were later than most babies, you slowly began to take back what you'd lost. You started to crawl, then to pull to a stand. I certainly wasn't going to tell you that you were not supposed to walk.

I called doctors. I called specialists. They said "How

interesting. How fortunate. We can certainly give it a try. It can't hurt. It can only help."

And so, the Tour de Hospital began. Therapist after therapist, doctor after doctor, Shriners', Primary Children's, Early Intervention, studies and camps, and orthotists – four, six, twelve appointments a month.

You got your first pair of SMO's, which did not fit in shiny black shoes, and in those SMO's, you stood for the first time. You took shaky, limping steps in a gait trainer, like a little old woman with a walker.

Then, you were fitted for your first pair of AFO's. Those certainly didn't fit in shiny little black shoes, but you took more confident steps.

The bills started coming in too. Three, four, and five figure numbers. Thank God for insurance.

But then there came the suggestion. There was a place, a place that teaches children who are not supposed to walk, that they can. I sent an email. I collected a few letters of recommendation. You were accepted to the program, aptly named, "Now I Can."

It was expensive, I couldn't pay for it. Another fit of ugly tears and some undignified flopping about, and your dear aunt waited patiently for me to grow up again and said, "We can do this. Let's find a way."

And so, we did. In the hot sun, five dollars at a time. We

made the money. And you went to "Now I Can." There, you took your first unaided steps. By the time we left, you walked out of the building under your own power.

It's been two years since the day that unseen force stole your legs, and one year since you, blind to the condemning prediction of men in white coats, unwittingly took them back.

Hundreds of thousands of dollars. Hundreds of hours, dozens of appointments, multiple rounds of equipment, and now you walk, you run, and you dance.

The shiny black shoes never did fit. You were meant to fill a bigger pair of shoes.

Love, pride, and awe,

Mommy

Different Abilities

My name is Sasha. I'm a 42 years old, single mother of three daughters. My youngest is Kai'Lani who has Achondroplasia. I am writing my letter to her.

My Dearest Kai'Lani,

I was so shocked when the stick showed two pink lines. I was getting older and had convinced myself it was the onset of menopause. How wrong was I? I was so excited. I was also scared. At 40, I was considered of *advanced maternal age* for a pregnant woman.

My pregnancy with you was fairly easy. I did have gestational diabetes, so I was on a special diet to keep us both healthy. I had all my sonograms and I had bloodwork to check for birth defects. Everything came back normal.

You were growing and very active, sometimes keeping me up half the night with your in-utero gymnastics, that should be an Olympic event. I was tired. A lot. I worked three jobs and had your two older sisters to take care of as well. Your sisters were so excited to have a baby sister on the way.

As your arrival date drew closer, my OBGYN kept insisting on a Cesarean Section, I did not want that. She was worried about you being a bigger baby and me not being able to deliver you the natural way. A *bigger baby*. Hmmm... remember that description. It will be ironic later in your story.

Fast forward a few weeks to February 2nd, 9:00 A.M. I was feeling a little off. My water broke! Time to head to the hospital.

I labored all day. The labor and delivery nurses trying every trick they had to help keep me from a C-section. It worked! You came into the world and slipped right into my heart.

There was something not quite right. You needed oxygen. You were short but had all these little chunky rolls (remember that term bigger baby).

You were amazing and beautiful but there was something, I didn't know just yet.

The pediatrician kept sending you for tests. Yet, she gave me no information as to why or what she was looking for.

Our second night in the hospital, they had sent you for more scans. At four in the morning, I was exhausted, but also so upset. I wanted my baby in my arms and I wanted answers.

A nurse finally brought you back to me and I carefully unwrapped your blanket and got you down to a diaper. I looked at you, so perfectly amazing. You looked back at me with your deep blue eyes.

I Googled. I know it isn't the best thing to do, especially when it comes to medical diagnosis. It hit me. A calming peace came over me. My heart swelled. I realized in those wee hour mornings, both of us sleepy and just staring at one another, that you were a Little Person (again remember that term, bigger baby).

I was not angry, but I was scared. For you, for me, for the

Different Abilities

journey we now both faced. I made a promise at that moment, bringing you to my breast to nurse, that mommy would be your biggest advocate and your biggest fan.

The pediatrician finally came in the next afternoon and confirmed what I already discovered on my own. The paperwork stated, "Suspected Achondroplasia based on shorter limbs and larger head circumference."

We needed to see a Genetics specialist in skeletal dysplasia to confirm. We did. Then the reality set in.

I had a child that was different, with needs I had no clue about. Achondroplasia does not run in our family, or on her father's side. It can just happen. A genetic mutation. I read up, I asked a lot of questions, and I joined support groups on social media. I will never stop learning about it.

You have a great care team full of specialists. We spend a lot of time in appointments or clinics and driving to the children's hospital.

You had decompression surgery at just seven months old, you were a warrior. You are a warrior. You must be on a pulse oximeter at night, with a nasal cannula as well, providing you with necessary oxygen for your sleep apneas.

At 14 months old, you still aren't walking... YET. But you will. You are just 16 pounds and 26 inches tall. You are smart as a whip, too. We have not come across anyone who is negative at this point. You are starting to look like a Little Person and not just a smaller baby.

We have a long way to go. More surgeries, more tests, and more doctors. We will learn to navigate this world together. I will advocate and educate.

We will have to make modifications to help you in certain places and situations. You are a dwarf. My Nugget. My amazing little warrior. My Tiny Superhero.

You have taught our family about differences and disabilities, and tolerance and acceptances, and love. Most of all LOVE.

I am so glad to be your mother.

With all my love,

Your Mommy

Different Abilities

Dear Sweetest Brooklynn,

You are my little Miracle, my little Wonder Woman!!

The day I found out I was pregnant with you it was one of the best days of my life.

It was a really, really, long nine months. We had a date scheduled for you to make your arrival into the world, but you had other plans and decided you were going to come the day of your sister's birthday party.

The first time I laid eyes on you my heart was so full. You were the tiniest little thing I'd ever seen, weighing in at just 5 lbs. 4 oz. I couldn't wait to take you home to your sisters and have our family complete. You are so very perfect and barely cried.

Slowly after the first week everything started to change. You got sick with a cold and we were going to the doctors every day to get checked out. You were fighting for about 5 days, and then one day you wouldn't drink, so I called the doctor and took you in again.

I remember driving to the doctor's office in tears because I could hear you struggling to breathe, you were crying, and I just kept telling you *we're almost at the doctor's... the doctor's going to help you.* The doctor's is only a few minutes down the road, but it felt like it took forever.

As soon as we got there, they took you in a room and instantly tried to take your oxygen reading, when they finally got a good reading it was at 64%, they called a crash cart and immediately called 911.

I just remember my head spinning as I watched them give you oxygen, you were turning blue and your oxygen was just dropping and dropping, no matter what they were doing.

We were rushed to the Children's hospital and brought into a trauma room. I don't remember everything from those moments, I just remember Doctors everywhere, machines beeping, numbers dropping, and then they told me they had to put you on a ventilator. Your lungs were shutting down and your body was filling with carbon dioxide. You were barely 6 lb.

I was so scared I was going to lose you. I was all alone, surrounded by Doctors and nurses, working on you until you became stable. That night was so touch and go.

There was an angel there with you, there had to be. You had the best nurses and doctors. One nurse stood over you all night *bagging* you, keeping your lungs breathing with every pump when the ventilator failed to do it. The doctor that had to intubate you twice, blindly, when you vomited into your tube and caused it to push out.

You spent eleven days hooked to a machine keeping your tiny lungs breathing, seven of those days you were paralyzed and sleeping.

I'll never forget the day you woke up and looked at me, the day they took you off the ventilator and your lungs kept

Different Abilities

breathing, the day I heard your cry again for the first time.

You fought for your life for seventeen days, and I will forever be grateful you did. Although you still face many struggles because of this, you are growing stronger every day. I can't wait to see you grow and have an amazing life, because you my dear, are a miracle.

Love,

Mom

Chantelle Turner

To my wonderful daughter Sophie,

I want you to know how lucky daddy and I are to have you as our daughter. Also, how lucky your little sister is to have you as a big sister. I am proud to be your mommy. You are a wonderful daughter and a great big sister.

I am so proud of how far you have come. You have made great progress. I am proud of how strong and stubborn you are. I love your little personality and the silly faces you make.

Your daddy and I are so very proud of you.

We always want the best for you in life. We will always love and care for you. We will never stop fighting for what is best for you.

No matter where life takes you, we will always take care of you. Never stop being you.

Love,

Mommy, Daddy, and sissy

Different Abilities

Dear Laurie,

As I watch you grow, I wonder how you'll be when you're older. You have come a long way since you were diagnosed with Sensory Processing Disorder and speech delay, when you were two.

You're about to turn five soon and you'll be starting pre-k in a few months.

You still have struggles to go through but just remember mommy is always right here with you every step of the way.

You are my world. I love you.

Love,

Mommy

Different Abilities

Chantelle Turner

Chapter 3

To My Partner

"Don't search for the meaning of life. Simply be present for the people you love."

– Maxine Lagace

To my wonderful husband,

I want to thank you for all you do for our family. Both of our girls are blessed to have you as their daddy.

Sophie is blessed to have a daddy that fights for what is best for her. You are part of her voice. You are always there for her when she needs you.

The sight of you lights up her face, all day, every day. She is a full daddy's girl, there is no question.

I am grateful to have your support in this crazy journey. I know sometimes it can be hard and Sophie can be a handful. I just want you to know you are doing a wonderful job!

I don't know what the future holds for her, but she has an amazing dad who will always love and care for her.

You will always be her voice, if she does not gain one, and even if she does find her voice. She will always know you

Different Abilities

love and care about her.

Love,

Your wife

Chantelle Turner

Dear Babe AKA Davey,

Thank you for being my rock. Thank you for letting me vent. Thank you for letting me cry.

Thank you for knowing when to listen to me and knowing when to talk.

Thank you for letting me be negative and thank you for hearing me when I want to try some crazy idea I've came across, because it might help our son.

Thank you for going to the pharmacy endless times and the grocery store to get soymilk for 100th time this month.

Thank you for loving me, especially lately when I've been hard to love.

Last, but not least, thank you for making this beautiful red headed boy with me.

He has taught me so many amazing things in the short four years he's been on this earth.

I love you with all my heart

Love,

Joy

Different Abilities

Dear Terry,

I don't always find a way to say the things I need to say, or the things I should say. Sometimes it is hard, even from the beginning our relationship was not a typical one.

Five and half years ago when we met, I had a son, Damian, who was only 4 months old. That did not bother you at all, but in the months that followed, we went thru a lot. There was the testing for Damian's health issues and then the car wreck, which could have taken you away from us.

As a single mom, the struggle was real, and trying to date was a challenge. I had a small support system, my dad, mom, and uncle, with a few friends.

Three months into our relationship, my son was admitted for testing and just like it was a natural thing, you automatically came and stayed by our side.

When he got sick and had his first set of seizures, our relationship hit a roller-coaster and fast, but there you were, every step of the way.

Together we learned he had Epilepsy, Chiari, Cerebral Palsy, and had become developmentally delayed. You helped us get to his doctor's appointment in Nashville and Chattanooga, and wherever we needed to be. You went to all appointments with me and wanted to help me raise my son.

Now we struggle with his behaviors and learning curves, and everything in between.

You even helped me when I got guardianship of my two cousins. You tell me all the time, "I am here for the long haul, the good, the bad, and whatever the world throws."

You have shown Damian that he can be whatever he wants, and do what he wants, so long as it doesn't hurt anyone or cause himself harm.

Together we have learned mental health challenges can be a tough pill to swallow, especially when our child has special needs.

Damian tells you daily that he loves you and he appreciates what you do. Even when you send him to his room, and he comes back and demands you tell him sorry, because you redirected him.

You tell him he is your son and he tells the world, you are his daddy.

Remember that night when he came to us and asked why his biological dad didn't love him, and why he stayed away? Together we told him that it was not his fault, and his biological dad does love him. You added that sometimes people need to love from a distance. Our 5 year-old pondered and he said, "I can do that too, thanks daddy."

You have been our rock, our safe place, and anywhere we are with you is home. Through the appointments, school meetings, and therapies, you want to be there.

There are no words I can use to really express to you the gratitude and love we have for you.

To the love of my life, the man that stepped up and stepped in, not knowing the rollercoaster we were headed down, THANK YOU from our hearts and from the skies above.

You always find a way to make things happen when we need

Different Abilities

to, and you always take care of our family first. Thanks for being my person.

Love you always,

Traci.

To my Partner,

It's hard to know what to write to you. I guess I'll start by saying I love you, and you love us.

Some people see that I deal with baby boy more than you. Or I deal with him better than you. This is true, but not because you don't try, not because don't want to deal with him. In our little family, we each have things we are best at. I deal with him more often and a deal better than you, but you work hard.

You do extra jobs to provide for us. When it comes to dealing with more stress with workload, bills, and planning vacations, you rock it. I don't deal with those things like you can, and you doing that allows me to focus on him and ensure he is well taken care of, learns, and grows.

We do things together as a family and we're able to, because I can deal with him more while you do the planning, and that beautiful balance is what makes it work.

When I do need a break, you're there. When I just need a moment to myself or even a night, you're there. For this I can never thank you enough.

When we get a weekend away, you're still working and planning while I'm along for the ride. This is so important to me and I love that you are willing to do it so I can relax and not worry, just for a little bit.

All my love,

Your baby

Different Abilities

Chantelle Turner

Different Abilities

Chantelle Turner

Chapter 4

To My Son

"We know what we are, but not what we may be." – William Shakespeare

---

Noah,

July 26th, 2014 was the day that changed my life forever, and for the better. It was the day I became your mother and I couldn't have been happier.

The minute I saw the doctor deliver you, I was so excited to see you, so healthy, tiny, and so handsome. When nurses laid you on my chest, I was so overcome with joy, and so many other emotions. I just laid there, held you tight, and soaked everything in.

Your big green eyes, long eye lashes, tiny hands and feet, along with such a contagious smile... I just stared in awe of you.

I was so much at ease when the doctor walked over to me and said, "the baby looks great," and my goodness you did!

I laid there in the hospital bed for hours just gazing at you, thinking of all the things I was planning to teach you. I wondered what your favorite food was going to be, your

Different Abilities

favorite snack, and what your personality would be like.

You were such a fun baby. I loved taking you to the park and placing you in the swing or sliding with you on the park slide.

You loved bath time. The smile on your face during bath time would light up the entire house, your dimples were enough to make me smile, and the smile would last all day!

During your toddler phase you loved toy cars. You were so in love with cars, and trains! It was so fun to watch. In preschool you adored Thomas the train, you loved everything about him.

Now you are so friendly to anyone and everyone. Your personality shines as bright as the sun, and it makes me happy to see you being such a good friend. Each day is a new adventure with you!

I love you being you, the most loving, sweet kid I know, and so very smart.

My heart melts when you squeeze my neck for a hug and tackle me to the ground, followed by a kiss on the cheek ending with, "You too," for I love you too. My bond with you is so very strong and can never be broken. You are my son, and my love for you is like the sky, it never ends.

You are so lively, energetic, and full of life. You keep me on my toes!! I can't wait to see what the future holds for you, just please don't grow up too fast. I enjoy every second of you being my little *iron man*, you will always be my little boy.

Chantelle Turner

I'm so glad the God gave you to me. You have taught me so much. Like patience, you have taught me to be a little more patient.

I am so proud of how far you have come in school, and I have seen your personality shine through. Always be a friend to others. I want you to never give up, and always remember, I love you no matter what.

I love you iron man!

Love,

Mama

Wil,

You are an amazing, fun, and loving 5-year old, despite your rough past.

You were born at 27 weeks in Mississippi, life flighted to the NICU at Ochsner in New Orleans, and ended up with NEC, but survived being a preemie with no long-term issues.

Your birth mother had brought you to the ER in Mississippi because you were seizing, and it seemed there were other problems as well. Child Protection services was contacted, and you were flown to us alone, to give you the best chance of survival. The hospital in Mississippi was very concerned you would not make it.

Once you arrived at the hospital where I work, and the full extent of your injuries were discovered, the doctors thought, if you did survive, you likely would not have a good quality of life.

It was discovered that you had a skull fracture, brain bleed, bilateral retinal hemorrhages, an old healing arm fracture, and a bedsore on your tailbone area. In addition, you only weighed 13 pounds – 13 pounds at 13 months!

You had been shaken, starved, had your head hit on something to fracture your skull, and who knows what other horrors you went through.

For reasons unknown, because I typically do not follow children in the PICU, I ended up on your case. I immediately contacted the child protection worker and tried to contact your mom. I was unable to reach her, but the Mississippi hospital provided us with your mom's work number.

Your mom did not fly here with you. Even though she claimed she had to work, there was no record of her being scheduled to work. June 25th of 2015 was the last time she saw you, her beautiful son.

Your birth name was Wilinton but I wrote "Wil" on the board in your room and that name stuck.

For some reason, I felt a connection to you. You were one of the hundreds of abused children I had interacted with over my 16 years as a hospital Social Worker, but there was just something about you.

I would get to work, hurry up and do my job, and then spend any spare time with you. Miraculously, you made it out of the PICU – you weren't out of the woods yet, but you did not need a trach or a g-tube.

After you passed your swallow study, I gave you your first bottle, your first bath, etc. I did everything in my power to show you love after all that you had been through.

You made it through all the medical stuff and on July 14th, 2015 you were transferred to another local hospital, who had pediatric inpatient rehab. You were unable to sit up, hold your head up, or hold a bottle – typical stuff a 13-15 month old child can do.

Different Abilities

Throughout your long hospitalization, I communicated with your amazing DCFS investigator, honestly one of the best I have ever dealt with! She started encouraging me to adopt you, I thought she was crazy.

I was redoing my house – DIY, and my fiancé and I were in the middle of planning our wedding which was 12/4/15. Apparently, the child protection worker had a crystal ball.

My fiancé and I visited you every night at the other hospital, we fed you and would put you to bed, we seemed to be the only consistent thing in your life.

The nurses and sitters came and went but we were there every day. The first day my fiancé Joe met you, he looked at me and said, "he is our boy – we are going to adopt him."

As you continued to improve, I told my mom that we were considering adopting you if the Judge and child protection would allow it. My mom thought I was crazy. She was afraid that you would have tons of medical needs that would stress my fiancé and I out before we were even married.

As a mom, she was being protective of her only child and was scared for me and the unknown of taking in a child that could have severe medical needs.

We knew you would have cerebral palsy but didn't know the extent of it. I told her that I just had a gut feeling you would be okay. Being the great mom that she is, she said, "Do what you feel is best, I know you will make it work."

My fiancé Joe and I remained in contact with child protection and as you neared your discharge date, a court date was also coming up. I asked my friends from work and my personal life to write letters to the Judge stating that they know you would be in great hands with us.

On August 20th, 2015, the day before you were scheduled to discharge from rehab, my mom, Joe, and I went to Judge Alfonso's court room. We presented her with letters from our friends and pictures of the three of us together.

She then did the unthinkable, even though we were not licensed foster parents, she let us take you home to complete the process. We lived in Louisiana, you were from Mississippi, and it was a Mississippi Judge. She was letting us take you home!!!

We had a quick celebratory lunch at Arby's near the court room and then rushed home to clean up our DIY remodel home and get one of the guest bedrooms ready for you. Luckily, my mom had a crib she had used for my step-nephew and the rocking chair she used to rock me in.

All my friends rallied to make sure we had everything we needed. One friend bought us a car seat, others brought over clothes and toys, we pretty much ended up with everything we needed for you.

My work also had a baby shower for us, you came to your baby shower! We actually didn't need to buy any clothes for you for about a year, of course we bought you cute stuff we wanted, but we didn't have to.

Different Abilities

Our friends and family immediately fell in love with and started to spoil you.

Joe and I immediately went to work for you. We jumped through hoops to get you in Early Steps, worked on switching your Medicaid from MS to LA, got you braces, got you on a waiting list for PT, OT, and ST.

Thankfully, a friend of mine owns a daycare very close to our house and she made a spot for you in the baby room. You were now able to sit up but that was about it, pretty much like a 6 month-old, although you were 15 months.

We made follow up appointments with every specialist who saw you while at the hospital where I work and luckily didn't need to continue to see all of them.

You did have a VP shunt placed while in the hospital because of brain swelling. Come to find out after several follow up appointments with neurosurgery, it was over-shunting and they clamped it off. You no longer needed a shunt.

You learned to walk with a walker and before too long, you were practically running. You also learned to take some steps without your walker.

Our little boy, who doctors feared would not make it, was doing amazing! Our lives got really busy with all of your therapies and our upcoming wedding.

You were a ring bearer in our wedding and were pulled up in a wagon, you could hear everyone let out a simultaneous *aww.* My mom and stepdad watched you while my husband and I were on our honeymoon.

As time progressed, my friend Kelley, who also happened to have a son with Cerebral Palsy, told us about a surgery called Selective Dorsal Rhizotomy. Since I had a medical background, but my husband did not, I had to encourage my husband to consider the procedure.

Before too long he was sold on the idea and we submitted paperwork to St Louis Children's Hospital, to see if you were a candidate. You were a candidate and on March 14th of 2017, you had your SDR.

It was the best thing we ever did, aside from bringing you home! You quickly stopped using your walker and started to use quad canes but quickly stopped using them as well. We happily donated your walker to your therapy center and passed the quad canes to someone else whose daughter recently had SDR.

With lots of continued therapy, your only remaining sign of having CP is drop foot on your right side and no arch on your left. Your right arm is also slightly weaker than your left, but you are doing AMAZING. Your therapists believe that once you are older, you will learn how to isolate the muscles that are causing the drop foot and strengthen them, so you no longer have drop foot.

You were adopted on November 7th, 2017, your bio mom signed her rights away voluntarily and an ad was placed to

Different Abilities

see if your bio father responded, but he did not. Joe and I were beyond thrilled and thankful that we could officially call you ours, there was no more fear in the back of our mind that someone could take you from us.

The Judge who let us take you home actually took a recess in her court so that she could see you once you were officially ours. She was glad to see a happy ending because she doesn't see them very often. Wil is now your legal name.

You have the best attitude, don't meet a stranger, and you're a little comedian. I am afraid for you starting school, I think you are going to be the class clown. Academically you are, for the most, on target but need assistance with writing and other skills like that. You will be starting Kindergarten in August.

You are also a big brother. You will be turning 5 on May 6th and your little brother Reid will turn 1 on May 11th. You are the BEST big brother, and I love watching you two brothers play and watching your love grow. Reid is always following behind you and you are always asking about your little brother, there hasn't been an ounce of jealousy since I gave birth to Reid.

I can't imagine our life without you. You've brought us and so many others, so much joy. As my friend once said, your worst day was also your best!

Love, Mom

To my son,

From the day you were born, I always knew you would be different. You came into the world early, but yet... still healthy. I watched you grow, and the more you grew, the more we learned that you didn't fit into the crowd.

Through all the doctors, all the pokes, and all the tears, you stood strong. Ten specialists and six therapists. When do we find the time to just let you be a kid? I have so many fears for you and how your life will be, yet when I look at your smiling face, they all just seem to slip away.

I just want you to know your diagnoses does not define who you are, you are SOOO much more. You are a beautiful boy. All the doctors would say, "He will never," but you still did.

In time, I hope the world around us learns to accept you, learns that you truly are an amazing soul, you just fight bigger battles. I pray that you have a true friend, I pray that you find somewhere to fit in, and I pray that the world becomes more aware.

I love you so much, more than you will ever know. I will never leave you, I will help fight these battles with you, and be forever by your side.

With lots of love,

Mommy

Different Abilities

Dear Hunter,

You are an extraordinary and amazing little boy.

The day mommy and daddy found out we were pregnant, was one of the best days of our lives. Everything we had prayed for was coming true.

For the next nine months you grew and grew in mommy's belly. Then the day we had waited for was finally here. We went to the hospital on the 8th and you made your grand entrance on the 9th at 6:53 pm.

It didn't go as planned, you were swept away from us too quick and we didn't know why. You were flown to OU Children's Hospital and that was our home for the next month.

On the 10th we received your diagnosis. You were born with Spina Bifida and Hydrocephalus. The doctors gave us the worst-case scenario and said you would possibly never walk or hit your milestones. They also told us you would have a low-quality life. As we were getting the diagnosis what we really wanted was our baby boy!

You went for your first surgery that day. They closed your spine and removed any exposing nerves. Mommy and Daddy was so excited and happy to finally see you. I'll never forgot at 5 days old I finally got to lift you and bring you in close. It was the best minute of my life.

You had to undergo another surgery just days after your first one, but you came out even stronger.

We got to bring you home on Christmas Eve, which was the best gift we could have asked for. Things got a little rocky and we were back in the hospital 3 days later. You had to go in for surgery one last time for your back, after that we were home free and for good this time.

As you grew bigger and bigger every day, we knew you were special and were going to do amazing things. That first year you hit every milestone and never gave up on anything you wanted. Time flew by and before we knew it you were turning ONE!!

Our little 8lb 5.3oz baby was turning one. We were ready for all the adventures you took us on, and you definitely took us on some amazing ones.

That next year you went under 2 shunt revisions, but the one thing that stood out that entire year was you started walking independently on your own. You proved the doctors wrong once again. Even the two surgeries didn't stop you from doing what you wanted and what you set your mind too.

You are now about to be 2.5 and you are the most spirited, kindhearted, loving, and always on the go, toddler. You don't let anything stand in your way of what you want. Even if it's just a candy bar. If you can't get it from mommy, you go to daddy and he gets it for you. You have daddy wrapped around your little finger.

Different Abilities

You and bandit, or as you sometimes call him bay bay, you two are a perfect match. They say a dog is man's best friend and with you it's true. You and bandit will run and play all day long, until one of you has enough and needs a break.

You don't like when we go somewhere, and bandit can't come, but as soon as we are home he comes running to you and sniffs and licks you from head to toe to make sure you are okay.

Mommy's new year resolution this year was for you to have an amazing year with no surgeries. Here we are almost halfway through the year and it's been amazing.

Hunter, no matter what life throws at you. We know you will always overcome it all. You have proven doctors wrong and you are still defying the odds. You are such a strong little boy, we want you to always remember that you are worthy, and you are more than your disability!

We want you to always be positive and never, and we mean NEVER, let anything stand in the way of what you want! Mommy and Daddy will always be right there rooting and cheering you on.

We will always worry about you, even when you are grown and have a family of your own. Not because you have a disability, but because you'll always be our little boy and that's our job.

When you think you can't do something, we want you to always remember you weren't supposed to crawl, but you did. You weren't supposed to walk, but you did. You were to have little to no movement from the waist down, but God chose a different path and we believe you were chosen to do something amazing in life.

Never say you can't do something because we know you can do it all if you want. Always believe in yourself like we believe in you. We will always be your biggest fans. Spina Bifida will NEVER define who you are or what you can do!

Love you more,

Mommy & Daddy!

Jayzen,

Oh, my boy where can I start.

When I found out I was pregnant with you I was so ecstatic. Your daddy and I were so happy to be having a baby together. The day we found out that you were a boy was the best day, except for one thing. The ultrasound nurse told us that the doctor needed to talk to us. I knew something was wrong.

I kept looking at the monitor with your sweet little face on it. I noticed part of your brain was black. I knew that wasn't good.

When the doctor came in, I told him to tell us what was wrong with you. He said you had a rare condition called Dandy Walker Malformation with Cyst and Hydrocephalus. We knew nothing of what that meant. He told us we had to deliver you in a bigger hospital because they were certain you would need a shunt.

April 22nd, 2013 mommy didn't feel good, but it was too early for you to come into the world, we still had a few weeks until we went to the big hospital. You had different plans. You were born at the hospital by us and had to be transported as a critically ill infant to Helen DeVos.

They wouldn't let me go with you, I had to wait 24 hours. When we finally got to you, you had an IV in your tiny little hands and in your head. Mommy cried. You proved all the doctors wrong and got to come home thirteen days later.

Chantelle Turner

You never needed to get the shunt.

You have given mommy a run for her money. You're sweet as candy and have an attitude like your daddy. With all the diagnoses you have, you're a strong-willed little boy who doesn't take no for an answer.

You are full of sass and know how to push my buttons, but I wouldn't trade you for the world little man.

I love you my superman

Love,

Mommy

Different Abilities

To my amazing Jasper,

At just 2 years old you were diagnosed with Autism. We had our suspicions at 18 months when you weren't making eye contact, you were not talking at all, and you played alone.

Finally getting a diagnosis means we get to help you in every way we can! You now attend Speech Therapy, Occupational Therapy, and ABA Therapy.

Now at 4 years old, you are smart, super lovable, and you don't want ~~for~~ much. Well, maybe some love and kisses, but besides that you're always happy. You like Mickey Mouse and really enjoy being outside.

While you do not like loud noises and are non-verbal, for now that is, you can communicate with your talker (Tobii) until the words come along. You also struggle with sensory issues, but you have a smile that makes others smile and you spread joy to those who help you. We are blessed to have so many, who love you so much, and want you to succeed.

I am always trying to learn about Autism and spread some awareness along the way, so I can help you, anyway I can.

I really want people to know that Autism is a disability that sometimes you can't see at first. Autism doesn't have a look; a person can't look Autistic. But a person with Autism may flap their hands when they are excited, or have trouble making eye contact. They may cover their ears when they get upset, or they may be wearing noise canceling headphones.

Chantelle Turner

I want you to know you are special, and we celebrate all your different abilities. As your mom, I will always be there to help you and help others better understand you. To help them know that if they learn the signs and symptoms, then they can have a better understanding of all the amazing people in the world around them, just like you!

You are special, you are deeply loved, and I cherish every moment I spend with you.

Love,

Mom

Different Abilities

Dear Baby Boy,

You are one of the most amazing people I know.

You fight hard every day to learn and grow, despite all your challenges. I know sometimes I lose my temper, and you can be stubborn as well. I want you to know that I will always love you no matter what happens.

As you learn and as you grow it will be hard, but always know I will never give up on you no matter how long it takes. I love your hugs and your kisses, and that beautiful smile. You find joy in the simplest things. You love and treat everybody equally. That to me is an amazing quality and I'm so glad you have it.

I want you to always stay strong and keep your head up no matter what the world has to say.

Love you forever,

Mom

To my son Kayden,

From the moment you were born I knew you were different. Not different in a bad way, just different. You were the only baby I knew that didn't want to be cuddled or touched, other than to be feed or changed. That never stopped me from trying though.

Then when you were one year and eight months old, you were diagnosed with autism. They said that you would never be able to fully understand things or take care of yourself. That you would always need someone there to help you.

From that day on I did everything in my power to make sure they were wrong. You went from extremely low functioning, to just low functioning. You went from not wanting to try to talk, to saying a couple words. You went from not being able to do things for yourself-, to doing things for yourself.

You have grown into this beautiful soul and I wouldn't change it. You are an independent toddler who is strong-willed and loves to laugh.

I can say in the past year you have grown and changed so much. It is amazing to see how far have come, given everything we have been through these past few months. You are still growing and pushing yourself, and I am proud of all the progress you have made. Yes, you will have challenges and obstacles-, but that has never and never will stop you from doing anything in life.

Never lose your compassion for others, you are the sweetest

person I know. You see the beauty in things and the good in people, hold tight to that quality.

I'm honestly excited about what the future holds for you, since you've exceeded the expectations of the doctor who diagnosed you.

You will always have autism but that doesn't define who you are. Autism is what you have and not who you are.

I will always be here for you and your brother. I know you will do great things in life. I am excited to see what you become.

Love always,

Mom

Elliot, my sweet little boy,

You have such an amazing personality. Your contagious smile and laugh just brightens our day. Your ability to build some very creative vehicles with Lego blocks or to combine all kinds of toys together in such a creative way, never cease to amaze us. Your excitement brings us and other people around you, you have so much joy.

To say that our daily life isn't challenging at times would be lying and deceitful. There are days where I am so exhausted, I no longer have the patience you need and deserve. Days where I simply feel so clueless. What am I doing wrong? What did I miss? What could I do better? Days where the guilt, and mostly the doubts, take over. Days where I don't know where to find the strength to keep pushing through.

Yet, while this journey is difficult at times, it is our beautiful journey. A journey filled with screams and tears, with doubts and fears, but also with smiles, laughter, tickles, runs, chases, stories, and games. A journey of progress and setbacks. A journey filled with colors and wonders.

Elliot, you are my teacher as much as I am yours. You teach me patience and hindsight. You teach me the value of the moment, and you teach me to see and feel the world differently and to embrace it.

The moment you were born, I knew how precious you were. What I didn't yet know was just how perfect you are. You are such a treasure to us, and we are very proud of you.

Different Abilities

I love you, always and forever. All day, every day.

Mommy (Mylène)

Chantelle Turner

To my little man Cameron Michael,

On December 11th, 2009 the first and only boy to ever have my entire heart came into this world. You completed our little family... me, you, and your big sister Sierra. Little did I know at that moment, you would have the biggest impact on me and change who I was as a person and a mother.

You were such a happy, easygoing baby. Amused by the simplest of things. You had more energy than mommy and your sister could keep up with.

As you started getting older you showed your independence more, and you pushed boundaries. You made it very clear what you wanted and let us know when you were upset or angry.

By 2 years old you were very stubborn, not wanting to be told what to do, and when or how to do it. It always had to be your way or no way. A lot of people told me this was the terrible twos and you were just being a boy, but as your mother I knew different.

Sierra and I had to learn alternate ways to help you get through your anger or tough times, and how to make you understand clear expectations and consequences. Each day was a struggle for us, but I know at that time it was even harder for you. There were days I cried and cried, asking myself why can't he just listen... why can't he just be good??

Then I learned just how hard it was for you to do the things we thought were so easy. Things were never easy for you. In

Different Abilities

2014 we got the diagnosis of ADHD and ODD. You were extremely hyperactive, oppositional, and defiant. It all made sense now. Mommy immediately read every book and every bit of literature on this, and used every training on ABA she knew, but things became difficult.

Your diagnosis was changed from ODD to Conduct disorder, because of the severity of your aggression and behaviors. At times I broke down and thought I needed to do better as your mother, I needed to be better for you, but never gave up on helping you be the absolute best person you could be.

School has always been hard... you were discharged from every daycare and summer camp you attended, but after finding the right school, the right medications, and therapies, you are now superseding everyone's expectations.

You are becoming an amazing young man Cameron, and I am so happy to be your mother. You've taught me more in 9 years then I could learn in a lifetime.

I've learned how to be patient and understanding in the hardest of times. You've taught me to slow down and enjoy life and the little things that make us happy. I've learned to love unconditionally and be thankful for what we have.

Cameron, no matter what anyone ever says in life, remember you are stronger and smarter than you think you are and can do everything you put your mind to.

You are perfect, and I wouldn't change a thing about you at

all. Sometimes I wish you could see yourself how I see you. Absolutely perfect in my eyes.

Continue to be the best you, cuz baby you are amazing just the way you are!!!

I loved you then, love you still, always have, and always will!!

Love always,

Mommy

Different Abilities

Dear Lucas,

My dear son, I want you to know mama loves you.

When I first found out you were going to be born without your left hand, I felt like it was my fault and I felt discouraged as a new mom. I thought about how it was for me, growing up with Sickle Cell, and it took me back to a time when I was teased. Every day you prove me wrong and show mommy you're just like the other kids and you can do everything anyone else could do.

At 3 months you were rolling over by yourself, at 7 months you were crawling. To think I had cried, because I thought you missing your hand was going to set you back. By the time you were one you could dress yourself.

It makes me proud that you're a strong person and I promise to always give you courage and be there for you. I'll support you in any way possible.

Just remember you can do all things you put your mind too. Don't EVER let anyone discourage you or tell you that you can't do things because you can, and you will go far as you want to in life.

Love Mommy

Letter to my baby boy,

Mijo, when you were three years old the doctor told us that you had autism. My heart dropped to the ground. I didn't know how to deal with it at the time. I blamed myself and God, but time went by I stopped blaming myself and God.

I started understanding and helping you. At times, you had your meltdowns in the middle of the store, in public. People would stare and point at us because they didn't understand.

Yes, you do have autism but that does not define you at all. You are more than your autism. I would like you to know that you have people that love you and care about you so much.

We are always here for you through the good and bad times. Yes, we have more bad times but that doesn't matter because our love for you is stronger than anything.

If I could, I would change the world for you my sweet baby boy. You are a loving, sweet, kind, and generous person. I thank God every single day that you are in our lives.

Love,

Mommy, Daddy, and family

Different Abilities

Chantelle Turner

Different Abilities

Chapter 5

To Those Outside

"In the end it's not the years in your life that count. It's the life in your years."

– Abraham Lincoln

To those outside,

Before I had kids, I remember being at a baby shower where we were playing games. One of the games listed all the letters of the alphabet and you had to find words related to babies or kids that started with that letter. I figured how hard could this be? Diapers, Crib, Pacifiers, Blankets. People would put different answers, and everyone would laugh and say, "That's not an answer!" It wasn't until I had my own children that I realized my answers wouldn't be typical either.

Apraxia. The term we would hear after almost 2 years of unsuccessful early intervention speech therapy with my son, the reason my son wouldn't find his voice until 3 years old.

Brushing therapy. Every 2 hours while my son was awake, I

would stop what I was doing to perform the Wilbarger Protocol. I would use a surgical brush to try and help regulate my son's sensory system.

Chewy tubes. Going through multiple different chewy necklaces, bracelets, and tubes, trying to find one that my son wouldn't chew through. He chewed so much that one Thanksgiving, he was so nervous he chewed right through his shirt.

Developmental Delay. The diagnosis that sits at the top of all my son's paperwork.

ENT. My daughter was 9 months old when we met our ENT. She needed ear tubes after recurrent infections. The specialist we thought would do a quick surgery and we'd be done with, turned out to be one of my daughter's favorite people to see these days. My son also needed a set of tubes, and my daughter is on her 3rd set at 6 years old. Our ENT helped guide us when we realized our daughters hearing was compromised. He removed both my children's adenoids and will be the one to take out my daughter's tonsils to help with her sleep apnea. So thankful for our wonderful ENT who has made each surgery a little bit easier.

Feeding Therapy. My son spent twice a week in feeding therapy trying to overcome his oral aversion. We tried to get to him to eat something other than crackers and chips. Crunchy foods are his go too. One of the happiest days was when they came out and said he tried a blueberry!

Gravitational Insecurity. We would learn this was the reason my son didn't want to lay on his back for diaper changes. He didn't enjoy swinging or going down slides.

Hypotonia. One of our newest therapy diagnoses, that led to us adding physical therapy into our weekly routine. It makes it hard for my son to do a lot of physical activity without wearing out quickly.

IEPs. Knowing my child will need extra help and trying to fight for that help within the schools. Hoping they will be allowed the accommodations they need to reach their goals.

Joint Compressions. I spend hours a day doing them to give my son proprioceptive input. We learned these would help relax him as well and use them as a calming method to help him fall asleep.

Kinesio Tape. His PT recommended we try Kinesio tape on his legs to help his knees from hyperextending. How cute a child can be with monkey tape all over his legs.

Leg pain. My son cries from this daily. His legs are a continued source of pain for him. He is wearing SMO's to help his ankles and hopefully help alleviate some of the pain. But until we find something that helps, we spend our days massaging his legs to try and help.

Meltdowns. One of the hardest parts of having a special needs child for me. Trying to help him find ways to calm down, to no avail. Watching him throw himself onto the floor or bang his head into things out of frustration.

Different Abilities

Watching him try so hard to catch his breath and stop crying only to have it start up again, until he eventually just wears out and falls asleep.

Neurosurgeon. We would have our first encounter with neuro after my daughter was born with Ventriculomegaly. Watching my tiny 8-week-old baby being strapped into an MRI machine to scan her brain was heartbreaking.

Obstructive Sleep Apnea. I will never forget the sleep study that led to this diagnosis for my daughter. It was such a long night. She was hooked up to so many wires and wrapped up like a mummy. She had a hard time staying asleep and I sat across the room watching her O2 drop throughout the night. We learned she has severe sleep apnea and she's scheduled to have her tonsils removed to hopefully help reverse it.

Proprioceptive input. A term we would learn early on in our journey. My son was always crashing into things, jumping, and wanting bear hugs.

Quick Shifts. Part of our sons therapeutic listening regime. We would sit for 20 minutes 2x a day and listen, to help him try and regulate. It would play over the car speakers on the way to the store to try and help prevent a sensory meltdown from overstimulation.

Respiratory Medicine. We were referred after my daughter had pneumonia twice in a year. I sat next to her while she underwent testing for cystic fibrosis. It's here we learned she has moderate asthma and severe sleep apnea. We would add daily Symbicort and a rescue inhaler into our diaper bag. We head to the doctor every time she has an upper respiratory infection, so she can start another round of steroids to help support her lungs.

Sensory Processing Disorder. My nemesis. The three simple words that make my sons day to day life so hard for him. Something that isn't even truly recognized by the medical community at this point but is oh so real in our lives.

Therapy. A place that would become our second home. I found friends who understood here. My son found therapist that he couldn't wait to see. We find so much support and help through therapy. It is also the place my son found his voice.

Understanding. Something I wish so much for my children. Special needs children are not scary. They are not weird. These children are amazing and loving. They don't see "different." And when my son was having a sensory meltdown in a store and I was told I was a bad parent; understanding would have gone a long way.

Ventriculomegaly. Such a small part of our journey, but it made one of the biggest impacts. Hearing during our firstborn's anatomy scan that she had enlarged ventricles in her brain scared me. My whole world changed. We were told to prepare for delays. Prepare for issues. I think maybe this helped me prepare for what would come later in our lives.

Different Abilities

Weighted blankets. One in the car and one at home. Always having one with us to help our son. Another part of his sensory regulation.

X-rays. We've undergone more than I can count. Bone age x-rays, x-rays for constipation, x-rays on her lungs. My daughter knows exactly how to get to the x-ray check-in now.

Yoga. OT would add yoga into my son's therapy. He now knows a handful of poses and we keep working on them to help strengthen his core.

Zantac. What both my children would be on to control their reflux. My son would go on it after being taken to ER for turning blue from coughing and gagging.

Those are my A-Z answers these days, and although my answers are not what most people would expect, this is my life. Some days are good, and some days are hard. Some days I'm so thankful for everything, and some days I have trouble finding the good.

But through all the days, one thing never changes. My children are amazing. They have taught me what it is to see the world in a different way. They have taught me compassion and understanding. They have shown me that even the smallest milestones are something to be celebrated. And most of all, I've learned that everyone has their own A-Z answers, and that doesn't make them wrong or different.

That is their story. Their normal. And they should all be accepted in the same way.

From, A Caring Mother

Different Abilities

Dear Friend,

I hope this letter finds you doing well, I want to let you in on a little secret.

I want you to know that it is okay to ask me questions and it is okay to celebrate your child! It is okay to find out what is going on with me, who knows maybe you can offer me some help. Even if it's just bringing me a meal, or coffee, or coming over to visit and talk.

It is tough for me to leave the house sometimes, but I do what is in the best interest of my child. I am not ignoring you or avoiding you, just as I'm sure you are not ignoring or avoiding me. I know we all have lives and it gets in the way, I am not mad or upset because I know how busy my life is with a special needs kid.

I'm at home giving meds, checking vitals, making appointments, calling the insurance company and doctors; or we are at a doctor appoint, therapy, or in the hospital. You are probably at work, cleaning your house, going to the store, or trying to keep your kids entertained. Some days that might be harder than what I am doing.

I am not going to lie; I wish things were easier for me and there are days that I wish my life could be more like yours, but I also know that we are all not meant to walk the same path. Spending a lot of time in the hospital and at doctors was not what I had planned for my life when I pictured my family, but also know that I love my children just the same as you love yours.

I want to see your child's accomplishments and I want to be happy for you. Your child's life is no less important than my child's life and should be celebrated as well. I may celebrate small steps, like when my child walks or figures something out, but I also want to hear about your child's straight A's or when they get an award.

When your child is sick or having surgery or needs a pick me up, let me know, I want to be there for your child, just as much as I want you there for me. Yes, my child may be medically complex, but sickness can strike any kid at any age, and it means a lot to me to be there for you as well.

I appreciate the help you do give me and the little things you do for me.

Basically, I want you to know it is okay to be different. I don't hate you for not understanding, I just want you to know that the best way to come close to understanding is to ask questions, to be informed, and to know that I want to be happy for your child.

You too are amazing!

Kristen

(mother to 3 super amazing kids)

Chantelle Turner

Different Abilities

Chapter 6

To Someone Who Needs to Hear it

"Lighten up, just enjoy life, smile more, laugh more, and don't get so worked up about things."

– Kenneth Branagh

When I found I could write an entry for this book, I knew I wanted to reach out. I knew I wanted to help another mama who was struggling emotionally. That could be you today, that might be you tomorrow. This special parent journey sheds a new light on the term *emotional roller coaster*.

To Someone Who Needs to Hear It,

I remember when we first found out my son was delayed at his 15-month well checkup, October 2016. Ever since that day our life has gotten harder and harder, but it's made me stronger and stronger.

My son was chubby and cute, he was healthy in every way, and the sun was shining outside. Life was beautiful... it still is.

To be honest, this week hasn't been a strong point. Noah

Different Abilities

was just diagnosed with Moderate ASD on March 13th, 2019. It's now been 2 weeks and 1 day since the diagnosis. I'm terrified of the future and bitter toward the ones who don't understand. I'm sad that some of my friends don't try to understand.

Please don't allow yourself to constantly try and inform people because, it's exhausting, and they may disappoint you. I'm frustrated that I need to *search* for ABA services, as if this journey isn't hard enough with a tight schedule, lack of sleep, and emotional plummets. You would think the least the universe could do, is put a paper in your mailbox with the vital information you need, explaining the process you're about to face.

Really, I just want my son to be **okay**. I'm hyper aware of adults with special needs now. I love them, I see they're beautiful, I'm proud of them for who they've become and what they've overcome.

I don't want my son to be helpless when I'm no longer here to help. I want him to know how to defend or protect himself and provide or pay bills.

If I died tomorrow in a car wreck, in some ways it wouldn't matter that he's on the spectrum, since he's only 3. Aside from the fact no one knows him like I do. A typical child of his age will still require another fifteen years of care and supervision. But, what about when he's 33 and still requiring care?

I'm very emotionally detached as I write this because if not, my phone would be soaked in tears and I wouldn't sleep tonight.

By now, I may have painted you a picture of all my fears but there are many positive things too! My son has never told my husband how much I spent shopping. He doesn't ask why repeatedly and never askes if *we are there yet* in the car. As odd as it seems, with him being so delayed, he's very adult-like and is often content sitting quietly away from the nonsense other toddlers can bring.

He loves puzzles and fruit. He can repeat so many words. He loves hats and I'm sure he will collect them when he is older. He's adventurous and he pulled me out of my PPD (Post-Partum Depression) when he was a year old, by crawling to the door and crying to go outside every day. He longed to enjoy the sunshine, daily, even as a baby, he got that from me.

He didn't walk until 18 months and is still having balance issues at almost 4, yet he won't stop trying to learn to climb. He's NOT a quitter. He doesn't care about materialistic things, a broken 25 cent helicopter at the thrift store brightens his day.

Best of all, he loves me. He just doesn't say it. He shows it. He cherishes me and I cherish him. Every mother loves their child, but I'm programmed to protect him. The thought of someone hurting him brings a tear to my eye and a fire to my soul. It's not an innocent motherly love. It's a fierce passion. And it's beautiful.

There's a lot to learn from people with different abilities and he teaches me new things daily. You're going to doubt yourself and you're going to face hard times, but I promise, if you'll just step back and look at the bigger picture, you will find your life is so much greater than the setbacks.

Well, honestly, this was supposed to be a letter and it turned into me jotting down the mixed thoughts and emotions I feel from day to day.

I hope if I've said anything of importance, I've shown you the bright side and the hard side of ASD. It's important for us to mourn. It's important for us to be honest. It's important for us to allow ourselves to feel the emotions that rise, and work through them.

But it's also important to remind ourselves that our lives aren't *bad*. They're anything but that. It's important we always embrace the positives and laugh at the goofy stories and situations that ASD brings.

I remember one time, recently at a park, I needed to go potty and my son was obsessing over the ducks in the pond. Chasing the ducks is an Olympic sport for him. He chases them until they jump in the water to get away. Then he laughs until he can't breathe (literally), and flaps uncontrollably. I sometimes think he wants to fly away too.

I was trying to stay within arms-length of him to ensure he didn't fall into the water. We were so far away from the car, and the civic center with the restrooms, I immediately started sweating and my anxiety started rising.

Panic was taking over because I knew he was going to highly protest, the moment I tried to pick him up and remove him. I was going to have to carry this 37lb screaming, flailing person, who is only a foot shorter than I am, a great length to get to a bathroom, and hopefully contain him in a stall to actually relieve myself. All this fuss, just for me to go pee.

When I took a moment to reflect on what was happening, I laughed. Sometimes life is like that. You just laugh at what comes your way. Take it second by second instead of hour by hour. In time, you'll make it to that glorious public toilet, or you'll pee yourself on the way, but you will survive.

I'm starting to realize the severity of our situation and I don't want to pretend it's easy. It's not. But just remember, you're strong. YOU can handle this life. I've had so many days where I thought I couldn't and wouldn't make it to the next day, but three days later I'll look back on those thoughts and I learn, once again, just how resilient we are.

My son is the best blessing I've ever received, and I will never give up fighting for him, he deserves my all. And, even if your child can't verbally tell you, they see you fighting so hard for them, they feel your love, and they're deeply thankful you're their mother.

With strength and grace, From one mother to another

Different Abilities

To all other parents of kids with special needs or those who work with them,

I'm a mom of multiple kids with special needs. Nevaeh is currently 10, Chip is currently 14 and Josh is currently 13. We homeschool them due to their high level of needs. They're all very sweet and tough kids. They've all endured so much and still, keep going.

They never lose their faith in God and neither do I, even during the toughest of times. That's what gets us through this journey. Our love for one another never fails us.

In case you're wondering, Nevaeh has been diagnosed with chronic abdominal pain, abdominal epilepsy with 2 types of seizures, asthma, reflux, allergies, heart murmur, immune deficiency, and the list keeps growing. She has had multiple procedures, infections, and surgeries. She also gets sick quite easily, so we are careful when around crowds of people. Josh has been diagnosed with asthma, allergies, epilepsy, and ADHD. Chip has been diagnosed with asthma, allergies, ADHD, and intellectually deficient.

You'd never know by looking at any of them that they have all of this going on, but they do. There's never a dull moment in our world, but we always stick together through it all.

Never let anyone tell you that you don't know what's best for your kids! Parents (especially us moms) are the first ones to know what's wrong with our kids.

Never let anyone get you down! Only you know your journey

best! Love, faith, and support can get you through anything!

I only hope and pray that my words have helped someone else out there.

Keep the faith!

Mary

Letter to Parent(s) of A Newly Diagnosed Child

Hello and welcome,

Your world has just been turned upside down, you are still in a state of disbelief, and have no idea what to do next. I remember feeling that way as if it were yesterday, instead of 16 years ago.

The first thing I want to say is welcome, the second thing is, I need you to take a deep breath in and now slowly let it out. You have just been given a diagnosis, an answer, not a sentencing.

Your child is the same child he or she was yesterday, today, and will be tomorrow. Remember that the diagnosis is just a label, it does not change the child you love and will continue to love.

The world that you planned for your child and family is still going to be great! It is just going to be different than before you received the diagnosis, and what you thought the future would be.

There will be days where you feel alone and that you just cannot do this anymore, it is alright to feel this way. Just remember there are many resources out there to help you navigate through all of this and be your child's best advocate. Many of these resources are at your fingertips.

Remember to take care of yourself during this journey. Unfortunately, parents will put the needs of their child ahead of their own almost every hour of every day. Please take care of yourself, take at least 15 minutes out of every day to do something for yourself. It may be something as simple as going in a room by yourself and taking some deep breaths in the quiet.

Chantelle Paige Turner started a group called Stronger Mommies. It is a group that helps other moms (parents) with the challenges of raising a child with special needs. The Stronger Mommies group is on Facebook™ and it has been an amazing resource for me.

Take care and enjoy the journey, it will be worth it.

Brenda

Different Abilities

Dear Stranger,

Perhaps your experience was like mine. I had given birth, but my baby had to be shipped to the nearest NICU that was an hour and a half away.

I had a wonderful pregnancy until the delivery when the Doctors had to put me to sleep and deliver my child. I am told he-was blue and lifeless, and the Doctors had to work on my precious baby for 20 minutes before they got his heart to start beating again.

When I woke up in recovery, I kept asking about my baby, but no one would give me any answers. When I got to the NICU, I heard doctors say things like "He has a 10% change of surviving this." I can still hear those words echo in my ears.

That was My Reality in July 2018. My son went a minimum of 20 Minutes without Oxygen and had to be brought back. He now has a brain injury known as Hypoxic Ischemic Encepathy or HIE. He isn't like average babies. He is gastric tube fed and has a Trach to help manage secretions. My Son has a high chance of getting diagnosed with Cerebral Palsy when he is older. We have no idea what the future has in store for our family.

I can tell you, while you may feel alone, scared, and feel like those four walls are closing in, on you and your little one, you are NOT ALONE.

I can tell you that the BEST thing I did, as cliché as it sounds,

PRAY!

I can't tell you enough how much I felt comfort in praying, then I would get on my social media and ask my family and friends to Pray. I've had random people hear our story and pray for my son.

I just want to say, while we may have these other things like a g-tube, a trach, and severe brain Injury, they DO NOT DEFINE my son. He does do much more than they said he ever would.

The second piece of advice I can offer is, celebrate every little victory. I know things may seem hopeless now but hang in there and follow your child's lead, it will get easier.

Yours Truly,

A momma who gets you

Different Abilities

To a new special need parent,

I remember vividly the day I took a pregnancy test, how elated I was, my husband and I were going to have our first child together.

I had dreamed my entire life ~~to~~ of have a beautiful daughter with dark hair, that would be brilliant. She would be a doctor or a lawyer, someone that would change the world, I was certain of this.

I knew SHE would be so strong, and though it may not have been the way I expected, she is writing her own story and changing the hearts and minds of everyone she meets.

At my ultrasound I was told I wasn't as far along as I thought, but I was positive. I had tracked cycles, marked calendars, planned, and prayed for this child. I knew the exact day she was made.

I remember trying to act like I might be wrong, thinking, and hoping I was wrong. She was measuring small and I knew that my life was about to look different than I had expected. I was assured by the doctors that it was fine, she was healthy, no big deal and I had nothing to worry about. I had an uneventful pregnancy, all the genetic tests we ran showed nothing. Everyone was expecting that I would have a perfectly healthy baby.

We set up the nursery, that we would never use, bought clothes, that we would never use, and started a baby book. We picked the perfect name and patiently waited for our little girl to arrive. And she did, a little late, which is what would be the story of our first year... everything a little late.

We did tummy time, we sang, we read books, we breast fed, we did everything we could, but the screens and questionnaires kept saying she was a little behind.

I remember being heart-broken, thinking that I have tried everything, am I not doing it right? I asked every doctor, went to every therapist office, trying to find answers that no one could give me, so I thought again, am I doing something wrong?

Fast forward several medical complications later, I remember my mother running into my childhood pediatrician in town and asking for answers that my daughters' doctors couldn't give. He mentioned that my child may have a syndrome. Everyone in my family and her doctors said it was impossible, she was beautiful, there is no way she has a syndrome.

In my heart, I knew she did. I spent countless nights staring at her little face wondering who she even looked like in the family. It didn't make sense. We decided to change doctors and try a pediatrician that was highly recommended by a special needs parent we knew. We had our first appointment, and it was decided that she needed a microarray.

The test came back right away, she was in fact missing a large portion of DNA. Her syndrome could explain her medical issues and why she had such unique facial characteristics. The results showed that she has a severe case and there was much more to come. This would not even be close to the end of our journey.

We would go on to have multiple surgeries, that resulted in her being tube fed. She also developed severe epilepsy with intractable seizures, that would also result in surgery.

That is just the beginning of her mile-long list of diagnoses. I have spent so many nights crying myself to sleep and asking why this had to be my child's journey, why we had to go through such terrible things together.

It wasn't until recently that I discovered my answer. This is not the life I expected, and there is nothing wrong with that, it can still be beautiful.

We live in a culture that tells us our kids should be this way or that, they need to be the smartest in class, the best athlete, and so on. It's heart breaking to think that your child may never be one of those. But I can say in confidence that my child has done and will do things that no other child could accomplish.

My child held my hand and comforted me when I cried as they wheeled her back to surgery. My child suctioned herself after a seizure when the nurse was panicking and couldn't figure it out. My child marches back to blood draws with her toddler head held higher than any adult there for the same thing.

She is a warrior, she is a fighter, and she will change the world. She has more courage in her tiny little body than any of us will ever know. She fights huge battles and comes out smiling. Now that I have met her, I can say for certain, she will change the world.

Sometimes as parents we blame ourselves. Was it because I took medication when I was pregnant, did I eat the right things, what did I do wrong? And it isn't your fault. None of it is.

Your child was given to you for a reason. And I don't think it's the cliché reason everyone off the street will give you... God gives his toughest battles to his strongest soldiers... I don't believe this.

I believe that I am lucky enough to witness one of God's miracles every day. My child has cheated death, she is strong, and a force to be reckoned with. She is a miracle.

Being a special needs parent is so hard, don't ever let anyone diminish that. With this life you might experience the lowest of lows that no one else could ever imagine, but you will also experience the highest of highs that no one else gets to experience.

I have never experienced the amount of joy I had when my child took her first steps, after doctors said she may never walk. I have heard her say *mom* for the first time, a few times (because of seizures) and I rejoice every time. You will get to celebrate accomplishments other parents don't get to enjoy. We just finished a 30-pound party for when she finally hit 30 pounds, after we tried so hard, for so long to get there. This life makes you realize that every day is a gift and the little things do matter.

So, celebrate your beautiful child that you waited for. A diagnosis is not your destination. Never (and I mean NEVER) limit your child, they can do amazing things if you let them show you. And if you let your child blossom into who they are, not who society says they should be, they will teach you so much more than you could ever teach them on this journey.

With understanding,

Someone who's been where you are.

To the newly diagnosed special needs parent,

I promise you it's going to be okay. I know you're overwhelmed right now, and this is a lot to take in, but I promise you will be okay.

When we got my son's first diagnosis, it was scary. It's scary not knowing what to expect or what will happen next.

One of the most important things I've learned is to let go of the expectations and learn he has his own timeline and he will do it when he's ready.

It was so difficult for me to watch my friends' babies hit their milestones, while mine wasn't. It was hard to see my friend's 8-month old standing independently, when my 10-month old couldn't even sit up yet. That doesn't get easier. But I've learned to focus less on what he would be doing if he were a typical kid and instead rejoice in his victories.

The first time he sat up on his own was the best day ever. It didn't matter that he should have done it months ago. It only mattered that he had made a huge step for him. Don't compare to other kids.

I know it's a lot. Doctor appointments, therapy appointments, and tests, seem to come one after the other. There were times I walked into every doctor's appointment terrified of receiving more bad news or another hospital admission. But I promise it gets better.

I've learned so much on our journey. I've learned to be my

child's biggest advocate. You know your child like no one else. Don't ever stop fighting for them.

Many time's the doctors have dismissed our concerns, but I always stand my ground. My son would have died if I hadn't spent 3 days arguing with anyone who came into his hospital room, until I found someone who would listen.

My child with special needs is the greatest adventure I've ever embarked on. I didn't sign up to be a special needs mom, but I try my hardest every day to be the best one I can be. He is the strongest human being I know, and he depends on me.

I know this is new to you and its confusing and scary, but please know that you are not alone. You are not alone, and you've got this!

Love,

A special needs mommy

Chantelle Turner

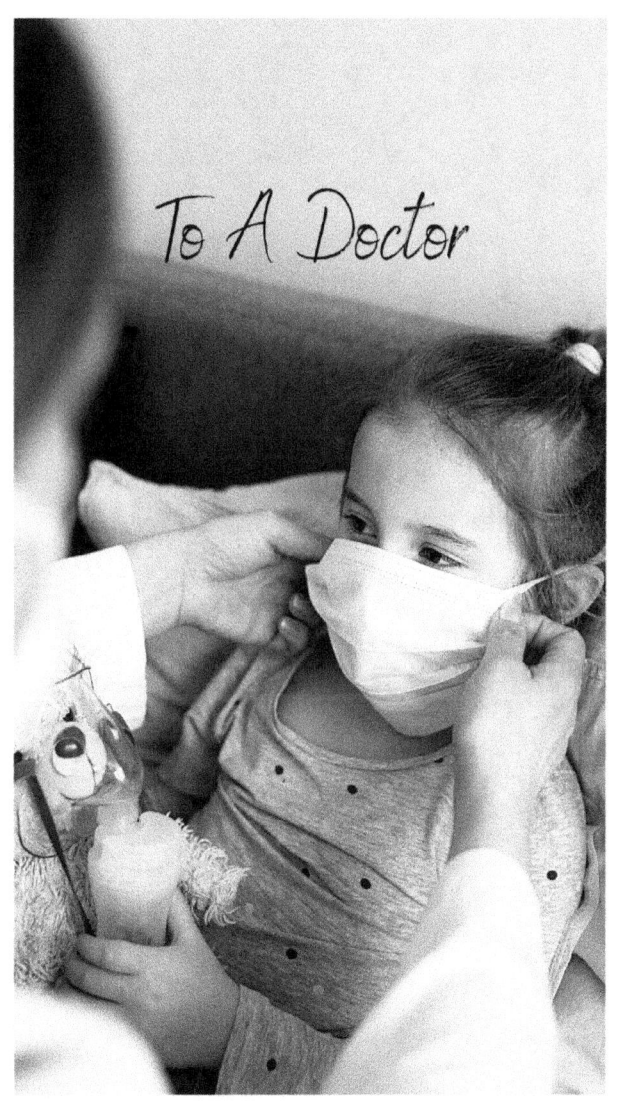

Different Abilities

Chapter 7

To a Doctor

"You only live once, but if you do it right, once is enough."

— Mae West

Dear Dr U,

You probably don't remember me; I wouldn't remember me. It's been nearly four years since I met you. John and I were at my doctor's appointment with our daughter Kaydence to find out if she was going to get a baby brother or a baby sister.

Dad and sister were so excited to find out we were having a boy and rushed off to tell Grandma. As I lay there and watched, I noticed they were looking very closely at my son's heart. John quickly returned to the room, leaving our daughter with Grandma. That's when you came in.

You told us that there may be something wrong our son's heart. You referred me to a specialist, who saw the exact same thing you did. He quickly started the process of making sure I had the safest and healthiest pregnancy and delivery possible.

Several doctor's appointments followed, and I had to travel back and forth from the hospital a few times. But on December 29th, 2015, I gave birth to the most amazing and perfect baby boy in the world. He was quickly rushed to be put on medicine to keep breathing properly and get him ready for surgery.

At one and a half days old he went in for open heart surgery. It was a very scary time, but I was surrounded by people who made me feel like everything was going to be okay.

He was supposed to be in the hospital for 4 to 6 weeks, but on his 1- week birthday, he got to move into his own big room. And on his 2-week birthday we were bringing him home!!!!

He is 3 years old now and you couldn't stop him if you tried. He is the most creative, sweet, caring, and brilliant child I have ever met.

He ended up with one paralyzed vocal cord... that's all... and is still the loudest child at any given event. And I have you to thank for this. For my beautiful child. If it wasn't for you, and your amazing staff it would have been a very different delivery, a very different outcome.

I thank you every single day for being such an amazing doctor and not stopping until you knew exactly what was going on with my son. He is absolutely, perfect, and I can

Chantelle Turner

thank you because you truly saved his life.

Always grateful,

Jessica

Different Abilities

Dear Dr. Kauffman,

My son Wyatt met you when he was only 10 months old. He was in Children's National Hospital in Washington DC. I was a scared, upset momma who was missing her other child. You came in to talk to us about our little boy needing a liver transplant.

I have always wanted to thank you. You were calm and listened to every concern we had. You spoke to us in terms we could understand without us asking. You spoke to my family and answered all our crazy questions. You even answered my daughter's questions, without hesitation.

When we had an issue, you fixed it without question and took us seriously. I will always be grateful for you.

During his transplant, you held my hand and made sure I was okay. After his transplant, you took the time to teach me how to care for him. I have never met a doctor so patient and understanding. I have emailed you about the craziest things and over-reacted to a couple things. You have been there for us through everything. Wyatt has come to refer to you as family, he looks forward to our visits.

So, thank you, from my family. I couldn't ask for a better doctor for my son. We truly love and appreciate you and everything you have done for us.

Sincerely,

Kristina and Wyatt

Chantelle Turner

Dear Dr. Lew,

I hope this letter finds you well. It's been almost 2 years since Zane's hemispherectomy, and life couldn't be better!

I want to take this opportunity to thank you for the meaningful and magnificent difference you have made in our lives. Thank you for sharing your skill and knowledge with the children you care for and thank you for being steadfastly by Zane's side throughout his journey.

You didn't just care for him medically, the humanity you showed and confidence you gave, carried me through as a mom. There was not a moment that I didn't feel as though everything and anything that could be done was being done. The team of talented and caring surgeons, doctors, nurses, and care partners were a constant source of encouragement and support during his 4 months.

I want you to know how grateful I am and how much Zane's life has improved! August he will be 2 years seizure free, he is off all seizure meds, both for the first time ever!! You and all the wonderful people at Children's gave Zane a new life, it is truly a special place filled with amazing people.

Thank you for saving my son!

Sincerely,

Kim

Different Abilities

To Dr. McDermott at Banner Children's Hospital,

The day our daughter was born and sent up to the NICU to be in your care, was one of the hardest moments of my life.

As a new mom, who's child was having complications with no explanation at the time, I was beyond overwhelmed. Not once in my life, prior to this moment or since, have I believed more than I did right then, that total strangers would take the best possible care of my child.

Everyone in the NICU was so kind us, but you Dr. McDermott did a favor for us that can never be repaid. You treated our family, complete strangers to you, like we had been your friends for a lifetime.

You helped us get in with an amazing Neurologist, Dr. Condie. It is my belief that by connecting us to him, you set our daughter up to have the best possible future. A future she might not have had if you had not made that incredible effort for us.

Now, 6 years later, our daughter does so many things they told us she might never do. She is kind, beautiful, and thriving because of that connection to Dr. Condie, his care, and the connections he helped us make as well. But it all started with you! You, your amazing NICU staff, and the outstanding care we received from you all.

With all the patients you see every day, you might not remember us, but we will forever remember you. You touched our hearts and gave our daughter a bright future.

Thank you will never be able to hold the love and gratitude I feel toward you, but I will say it anyway.

THANK YOU!

Chantelle

Different Abilities

Dear Dr. Scott,

I am hoping this letter finds you okay. I felt the need to write this out because some words need to be said to you.

You are an amazing person, surgeon, and doctor. I may hate traveling so far but there is no other doctor I would do it for. Going to the docs is never a fun day however, we never mind it much when we are going to see you.

What you do for kids and families just amazes me in every way. You helped us when we thought there was nowhere to turn. You took on my son when we were sent away from another ENT doctor.

We owe you more than this letter but it's what I can give. You saved my son's life.

You performed a surgery so rare you had to take time at home to sketch up a game plan on what to do. You have performed all his surgeries thus far and he isn't even a year old yet, with 3 under your belt.

We refuse to go anywhere else. We will always keep you updated with him and send Christmas cards. I have cried a lot in the hospital and probably will a lot more, but I always feel my son is in safe hands with you and I never trust people with that big of a thing.

You hold my son's life in your hands, and have a few times, with more to come. Thank you, Dr. Scott, from the bottom of my heart for healing and helping us as a family.

Chantelle Turner

Sincerely and never enough thanks can be said,

Brandy, Sam and Riley

Different Abilities

Chantelle Turner

Different Abilities

Chapter 8

To the Person Who Made a Difference

"You must be the change you wish to see in the world."

– Mahatma Gandhi

Dear random lady at the grocery store,

That day my son was having a meltdown, screaming in the cart, he was three, you kindly picked up his sippy cup and handed it to me. You saw how disheveled I was, the black circles under my eyes, the panic, and fear within them. You could see I was beyond feeling embarrassment.

That feeling had faded with each instance it happened and came to a skidding halt with a diagnosis just weeks prior. You saw into the very depths of me and saw great sorrow.

You gripped my shoulder and squeezed it as you handed me the sippy cup and you said, "It will get better, I promise."

You gave me a knowing smile. Then you went on your way before my eyes turned to daggers or I lashed out with words.

How would you know? Did you have a child that has special needs?

It may never get better, so how dare you say that. It could always be this way, the same meltdowns when he doesn't get his way, screaming, screaming, screaming, at the top of his lungs, and people judging me as a parent.

To be honest, I resented you that day. Your words haunted me and made me cry many nights. It may never get better than this. How would you know?

Days passed, then weeks, diagnoses were given and altered, therapy was non-existent due to lack of funding or qualifying. I put my all into learning therapy myself. I tried and tried.

My son grew and grew, in mind, body, and spirit, and language came. With the ability to voice his wants and needs, the meltdowns quickly vanished. With communication, the social aspects improved. Finally, recently, we got funding for therapy, and I can take a break from all the stress of trying to run two careers, be a mother and wife, and a therapist.

You knew, lady in the grocery store. You may've been able to tell my son was special, most likely not, but regardless you knew all children, no matter what, will improve. It may only be a little, it may be a lot; it may happen quickly, but it may take a lifetime. But you were right. It did get better. I wish I would had believed you then. I wish I could've seen past my exhaustion and despair, to see the wisdom and kindness in your words, make myself believe them, and look brightly toward the future.

Four years later, I hear you. I appreciate your words and they have stuck with me. It will get better has been my mantra, because every day, it gets better.

Yes, there will be setbacks and bad days, but each day even the smallest improvement is a cause for celebration.

I want to thank you today for saying that, as I should've then, because you've truly helped me turn my mentality around.

You were a mom assuredly telling another mom that it will get better because you knew that's what we moms do, whatever it takes to make it so.

Thank you.

Sincerely,

Lisa

Different Abilities

Mona,

It's so hard to find the words to say Thank you. You have meant so much to us; we owe you the biggest thank you. You're enthusiastic, kind, and loving, and we will miss you beyond words. Here's what we want you to know.

Thank you for every single IFSP meeting. Boy, we've spent time around that table. You worked tirelessly to create a plan that helps him succeed.

You have been his champion and advocate as much as I have, and I can't imagine going through this process in the future without you.

I know teachers are slightly filled with dread when it's time for another endless round of IFSP meetings, but you've always made them positive and encouraging, and I've left every single one, feeling incredibly proud of my kid's achievements and hopeful for his future. I think you might actually be Wonder Woman.

You do this ALL DAY!! Not only do you deal with my kid stalling and whining, you've got other kids doing the same thing and yet, you keep going with a smile on your face. I don't know where you find your endless reserves of patience, or how you stay so adorably perky, but I'm in awe of it. If you don't already have a superhero cape and a tiara in your supply closet, you deserve one.

Thank you for believing in my kid!

Honestly, sometimes you've believed in him more than I did! You saw that he was often capable of doing better, and you would create a learning plan, or a reward system, or any number of things to help him reach his full potential. And I'll admit, there were times when I thought, "He can't do that! That will never work!" But I was wrong, and you were right. And I'm awfully glad that I trusted you.

Thank you for loving him.

I know teachers care about their students, but I truly believe that the bond we've formed over the year is special; I believe that you have played a huge role in every achievement he has made over the last year. The fact that you are spending your own time thinking about the great week my son had, or worrying about why he struggled, shows a level of caring and dedication that I would never have expected, but I appreciate more than I can tell you.

I know he will have wonderful teachers, but there will never be anyone like you.

THANK YOU

Smith Family

Different Abilities

Chantelle Turner

Different Abilities

Chapter 9

From Family

"In three words I can sum up everything I've learned about life: It goes on."

— Robert Frost

My Precious Bethanie,

In the summer of 2017, I found out your mom was pregnant with you. There were so many emotions with the news, but the best was just how excited I was... she was going to be a momma, and I was going to be a NANA!!

I live a couple of hours away, so in the beginning, I had to watch her growing belly through photos or video, and occasional weekend visits.

I drove over, early one morning, to be present for the 4D Ultrasound where we discovered she was going to have a little girl! I was ecstatic... and so was your mom! We took gender reveal photos that same afternoon.

The feelings I had watching my daughter... my first born,

prepare for motherhood is almost indescribable. I was excited, nervous, and happy… those feelings just became stronger with each passing day. We were finally able to shop and decorate; we texted back and forth all day tossing around baby names. We could not wait to meet you!

The day your mom went for her 20-week visit, the anatomy scan, I was unable to go with her, so I patiently waited for a phone call or texts with pictures.

I finally got the call. I could hear in her voice that something was not right. She began to tell me, *they found something wrong with the baby's brain. It looks like the left side is not developing or possible fluid on the brain.*

As we talked on the phone, I was doing my very best to stay calm for her. I encouraged her to go ahead and call to make the appointment with the Perinatal Specialist. I assured her I would take off to go with her and we would do whatever we needed to do to help.

I hung up the phone and my heart sank. I was at work and had to walk away to just let it out. My heart was broken for my daughter and now, new emotions… fear, worry, and anger… why?!?!

Ashley had to start seeing the Perinatal Specialist on a regular basis… every 3 – 4 weeks, having tests run, seeing one doctor after another, and even counseled by a Genetics Counselor. She drove the two hours, every three weeks, to stay the night at my house, and then we would go to the appointments together.

You see, your daddy had to work, so my way of thinking was, I'm not going to allow my daughter to have to face any of this alone.

Whether it was tests or just a check-up... good news or bad news, she would never have to face any of it alone. Not to mention, two heads are better than one. I helped with questions, listened to doctors, and took notes. We wanted to be informed, at all times.

Before I continue, let me tell you... when a doctor says, *it could be, we think it might, there's a chance of...* it makes you question and want to do research. In this process, I have discovered that Google is a wonderful thing... and a terrible thing. Lesson learned... ALWAYS ask questions, take lots of notes, and keep ALL your office visit notes!!!

Ashley finally came up with a name... the perfect name for you... Bethanie!! We were told time and time again by one doctor after another, you may never sit up, crawl, walk, or feed yourself ... you would need constant therapies and need medical supervision for the rest of your life.

We continued with this prognosis, however, your mom and dad, and their huge support team did not give up! I am a firm believer that miracles really do exist!

At 38 weeks, the doctor did the ultrasound and told us, it was time for you to come. We were so excited... and a little nervous... but could not wait to meet you!!

Different Abilities

January 11th, 2018, you were born. I can still remember your sweet little noises and you smelled so good. This Nana was in love!!! I knew that there was a long road ahead for your new family of three, but at that moment, I was just so happy and relieved that you were here, and you and Mommy were doing well.

When you were 2 weeks old, you started seeing many different doctors at Texas Children's Hospital in Houston. You also had therapists that came for home visits twice a week.

For the first year, the best diagnosis that we could get was a Brain Anomaly. There was a great deal of uncertainty and a lot of questions, with no answers… simply a *"let's monitor her and check back in a few months."*

At a year old, they were finally able to give a diagnosis… Hemiplegic Cerebral Palsy, meaning paralysis on one vertical half of the body or weakness on one side of the body. The left side of the brain was the side affected, so the weak side is the right.

Your Neurologist, Dr. E (the ABSOLUTE BEST) keeps saying how surprised she is with how well you are developing. You have a great team of doctors that are taking care of you, and it shows!

You have limited use of your right arm, hand, and leg, but let me assure you, it hasn't slowed you down!

With each new day comes new obstacles. It started with

rolling over, sitting up, and feeding yourself. Almost daily it is something new. You're starting to talk, you blows kisses and play peek a boo... you've learned to kneel, have the cutest little army crawl, ever, and the therapists will soon start working on standing.

I have learned so much with this. The relationship between my daughter, and I is stronger than ever! I've learned to trust and believe in Medicine, in Doctors, but most of all, in Miracles!!!

You're now 16-months and prove daily that miracles exist. You are the happiest little girl and have the sweetest spirit. You love playing in the water and your absolute favorite... The Wiggles!!

Bethanie, I know without a doubt, your story is not over! CP does not define who you are, and you will continue to grow and flourish. There will always be obstacles, but nothing you can't overcome!

I am beyond proud of who Ashley has become... as a daughter, as a friend... as your Mommy. I know that this is what she's on this earth to do... to love and care for you. I am so excited to see all the great things you will do to contribute to this world.

I love you more than you will ever know!

Love, Nana (Jennifer)

Different Abilities

Brynn,

You were born a happy, healthy little girl... or so we thought. Defiantly happy, but not so much healthy.

At just a few weeks old, you were admitted to Children's Hospital of Buffalo with what appeared to be extreme jaundice. After some testing, we come to find out you have a gene mutation called Alpha 1 Anti-Trypson. It's a liver and lung disease and you will eventually need a liver transplant.

That hasn't stopped you though, beautiful little girl. You love to run, play, and jump. Jumping is your favorite thing to do! You can actually jump with one leg and the other crossed as if you're sitting.

You started to develop normally. Clapping, waving, saying Mama, Dada, Sis, hiya, bye-bye; and one day at around 10 months, you woke up and had forgotten everything you knew. It seemed as if you couldn't learn, couldn't speak, just stopped everything.

So, we had you evaluated by 3 different developmental specialists and sure enough you were diagnosed with level 2-3. Nonverbal autism, some developmental delays, and severe sensory issues. But again, this doesn't stop you.

You find many ways to communicate and get your point across. You're such a happy, content little girl, and we wouldn't change a thing about you.

The Lord has brought you to our family for a reason and we

love you so much.

Love,

Grandma

Different Abilities

To Margielynn, Jacqueline, Mauricio, and Maryah,

I want to tell you all to reach for your dreams and follow your hearts!! You can be anything you set your minds too.

We've struggled over the years, trying to decide what is best for you all and it has been hard. But I want to thank you for letting me be your Bitbit.

Jacqueline and Mauricio, you learn differently but it's going to be okay, we've got this.

Margielynn, one day we will get your ADHD under control. Maryah, always remember that we love you.

Sincerely,

Bitbit

Chantelle Turner

To My Bunny,

From the second you entered this world you've been a fighter. You greet each day with a smile. You are the strongest most resilient little girl I know.

Your journey has been rough, but you've never given up and I know you're going to change the world! We can't wait to see you blossom once you have your new liver.

We will be here for you through every challenge, to celebrate every milestone, and to give you all the love!

Good luck on Friday.

We love you,

Aunty Courty

Different Abilities

Remi,

Being a twin is a special thing. Being a twin to Kennedie, makes that position even more special. There will be times you feel like her best friend, times you are her protector, and sometimes when you feel overshadowed.

I want you to know how amazing you are. Even when you feel like Kennedie is getting all of the attention, you still matter to all of us! We will always be here to love on you, play with you, or just for a hug.

Your goofiness, happy personality, and electric energy make you such a special boy; and Kennedie is so lucky to go through life with you as her counterpart!

I love you,

Aunty Courty

Chantelle Turner

Colton,

What an incredible big bother you are! This past year has been hard, but you are always helping your mommy and daddy or playing with your brother and sister.

I know this past year was scary, sad, lonely, and sometimes not fun. We will always be here to help you through these times, so you never have to deal with anything by yourself.

You've proven time and again, even though you're just a kid, you are patient, loving, kind, helpful, and sometimes the best medicine for all of the challenges your family has faced. Keep spreading your love and being the best big brother!

I love you,

Aunty Courty

Different Abilities

Emily,

As you head into what is bound to be the most daunting and terrifying weeks of your life, remember you are loved. Your strength, courage, and perseverance over the last year as been nothing short of extraordinary.

Kennedie is so lucky to have you as her mommy, fighting for and loving her, as no one else can.

Always know we are here to help in whatever way possible. Whether that's game nights, watching the boys, or just for a good cry; we're just a phone call away.

Your little girl is a fighter and is going to come out of this stronger, healthier, and ready to take on the world!

I love you,

Courtney

My sweet Annabell,

Your entrance into this world was the most amazing thing I have ever witnessed in my entire life. You came in just screaming and so beautifully pink... my first thought was, *she looks absolutely perfect, how could anything be wrong?* The reality was there was something going on inside your small body with that tiny little heart of yours.

I've never seen so many nurses in one hospital room in my entire life. The truth was you were fighting for your life, and your parents were facing something uncontrollable. My heart was aching for each of you and would just keep aching more and more as time went on.

Everything was happening so fast. Your mother got to hold you for maybe an hour before they had to whisk you off in the helicopter for Children's Hospital. My heart ached because you were separated from your mother so soon, but dad, Mimi and Papa were right behind you while I stayed with your mother.

There were no words for what I was feeling in that whirlwind we were expecting, but never could have comprehended until it was actually happening. And I prayed like I have never prayed for anything in my life.

When your mom arrived at your location the next day, she was so excited to be with you, and I wouldn't have dreamt of being any other place.

When the diagnosis came in, it was better than the worst

outcome we could've been handed. We would have to wait a week for you to be strong enough for surgery.

There were so many doctors and so much information to take in. Even though the outcome was a good one, my heart ached for you and your family. I still knew God was in control.

For the week while we waited, I stroked your head with my finger and whispered how much you were loved, how beautiful you were, how strong you were, and how much we were praying for you.

I was amused by how hard it was to make my mind believe what my heart knew, you were a very sick little girl on the inside but on the outside, you looked amazing and very healthy. That was the first time I think it sank into my soul how different things really are if people would just take time to realize... things aren't always what they seem.

Your surgery day came, and we were all pleased to hear things went wonderfully. Everything wasn't completely repaired but everything that was life threatening was fixed. What a relief!!

You had a setback during transport between floors, which resulted in an extra stay period and take-home meds, but we were happy to accept that too.

During this journey of yours, you have taught me many more things than could be mentioned here. My belief is God knows what we need and when we need it, you're always where you're supposed to be, when you're supposed to be there, Gods timing is perfection.

As I went on this journey with you and walked those halls countless times, I saw and talked with so many other families. I realized there are many more people suffering than most can comprehend. My compassion was overflowing for each one.

Feeling helpless as a parent during normal everyday situations can be rough, but that was a whole new level of helplessness. I had to be the rock that wouldn't waiver for your mother, when all I wanted to do is find a quiet space and cry like a baby and you showed me that strength.

You were my rock that wouldn't waiver, because when I looked at you, I realized the only person in the room who was going through anything was YOU. There you were, without a care in the world, no idea what was about to happen to you, smiling up at me with bright eyes.

You ARE my realization of truth, my reason for more compassion, my talk with God, my something stronger, my bravery in the dark, my hero, and so much more. We're all in this together, from day one, I have walked beside you.

Almost 5 years later, I'm still walking beside you and will continue to do so for as long as I'm able. You are small, you matter, and you are important.

I love you

Different Abilities

To the newly diagnosed special needs parent (s):

I'm writing this letter from a grandparent perspective, with a special needs' grandson. Where do I begin.

First, the feelings of helplessness for my daughter, who is a single mom, and who deals with his issues 24/7. And then for my grandson who has no control over his actions and just wants to be like all the other kids.

I've learned from my daughter that you just can't give up. They're depending on you. The frustration is sometimes unbearable and yet the rewards make it all worthwhile.

Finding the right doctors, the right medications, the right school, and it goes on and on. It takes a village to raise a child and yours has special needs. We have learned that no one has all the answers and each child has their own special needs. No two are the same and sometimes you just have to follow your instincts.

We still have tough days, but things have really improved. He's happy and healthy, and doing great in his school. What more can we ask for?

My advice to you is, take one day at a time, the good with the bad, and know that you need a plan and a team, to help you get your child on the right track. Whatever it takes, they're counting on you.

Wishing you the best always, Kathy

In honor of my grandson Cameron. Mimi and Pop Pop, love you more than you'll ever know.

Different Abilities

Contributors

The following is an alphabetical list of all the people who contributed a letter to this book.

Alyssia Wilson

Andrea Z

Angela Corbett

Ashley Escalante

Ashley Robinson

Ashley Stone

Brandi Clay

Brandy Beauchesne

Brenda Marshall Olson

Brooke Rady

Cassie Wood

Chantelle Turner

Chelsea Ryan

Cloresa King

Deanna Novotni

Deanna Young

Emily Knakmuths

Different Abilities

Henreshia Hudson

Holly Anderson

Holly Rowe

Jennifer Elrod

Jessica Penwarden

Jessicalee Darling-Lima

Kathryn Knott

Kathy Heulitt

Kelli

Kim Iagroone

Koressa Avant

Kristen Wing

Kristina Brown

Lesley Marino

Lisa Graves

Maria Todaro

Mary Beadenkopf

Merle Horvath

Michelle Hoover

Mylene Cusson

Chantelle Turner

Paige Heulitt

Rachel Ferguson

Rosabelle Miller

Samantha Dalba

Sasha Albright

Shamsia Haque

Stephanie Stewart

Y Garcia

Different Abilities

Chantelle Turner

About Chantelle Turner

Chantelle Turner began her online entrepreneurial journey shortly after having her first child. Due to complications at birth, Chantelle was working hard to get her daughter the medical services and support she needed.

As she found ways to help her own daughter, Chantelle realized many other parents, who have kids with special needs, were not getting the support they needed.

So, with her learned internet and marketing skills, she founded her company; Stronger Mommy, with the mission to help special needs parents get the resources, services, support, and community they need.

While building Stronger Mommy, Chantelle found and developed highly effective strategies, that not only grew her group (Stronger Mommies) and her brand but became a movement.

Today, Chantelle runs several online projects as a coach and consultant, helping other business owners create a movement around their message. She is a speaker and best-selling author.

If you have a child with *different abilities*, Chantelle would like to invite you to come join the movement and the Stronger Mommy community!

www.facebook.com/groups/strongermommies

Chantelle Turner

If you're looking for more resources and support for yourself or your child, check out www.strongermommies.com

Are you ready for my next book?

Coming Soon!

Do you want a sneak peek? Keep reading for a BONUS chapter from my new book.

Introduction

The Emotional Rollercoaster of Parenting A Child with Special Needs

Recently we've been working with our 4-year-old daughter on understanding the difference between daytime and nighttime. She used to wake up almost every night in the middle of the night, and that would turn into hours of meltdowns, which ultimately resulted in a lack of sleep for both of us. In an effort to not lose my sanity completely, I finally gave in one night and brought her into our bed.

Before you start to judge my parenting skills in your own mind, let me just tell you that prior to this moment, I was 100% against ever letting my child sleep in my bed. I'll even shamefully admit I internally judged other parents who allowed this. So, I get where you're coming from if your reaction is not one of empathy in this moment.

Both fortunately and unfortunately for me, my daughter instantly went back to sleep in our bed and I even enjoyed getting to cuddle with her. Sadly, this was not to be a one-time occurrence. What had started in my mind as a single night, where I would catch up on some much-needed sleep, quickly turned into a nightly routine. Each night my daughter would fall asleep in her bed, only to wake up around 1am crying for me. I would get up and bring her into our room and back to sleep we both went.

Now, we've been working really hard the last several months to get our daughter to sleep all night in her own bed. The success of this has mostly come from helping her understand, that when it's still dark out, it's still nighttime and at night we sleep in our own bed. I've been blessed that most nights she's been sleeping until about 5:30 or 6am, which is when I typically get up anyway. On the nights she has woken up and wanted to come in my bed, I remind her it's still nighttime and with some minor back and forth, she goes back to sleep.

On the weekends, like most Americans, we like to sleep in until 7am or so, but by 6am the sun is up. Our solution to grabbing an extra hour of sleep, after the sun rises and our daughter gets up? Youtube! That's right, bad parenting moment number 2, we gave our 4-year-old an old iPhone we no longer use, so that she can watch Youtube while we sleep a bit longer.

Before I continue, its important I mention that my husband travels for work about 80% of the year. He's frequently gone anywhere from 3-10 days, home for a few days and then gone again. At the moment, he's been away for work approximately 5 days, so this week I get to play single mom.

One Saturday this winter, I remember thinking that sleeping until at least 6am really shouldn't be an issue. Sadly, the life of a parent is not as predictable as the sunrise. 4am comes around and my daughter is wide awake! I manage to convince her to rest in her room for about 30 minutes, by showing her it's still nighttime out, before I cave and let her watch Youtube early.

As 7am rolls around, so does the realization that my daughter has been watching Youtube for close to 3 hours now and I get to start my day off feeling like a bad mom. I roll out of bed, get myself and my daughter ready (never an easy task), and head downstairs to make breakfast.

My daughter has Cerebral Palsy (CP), Sensory Processing Disorder (SPD), Seizures (though we have been fortunate to be seizure free with medication for a few years now) and several other yet to be labeled challenges. I'll save you the long version but after a perfect pregnancy, our daughter had an in-utero stroke at birth. We spent a total of 11 days in the NICU, the first 3 of which we had no idea what was wrong with our daughter. When we did finally receive her diagnosis, it was done in the worst way possible. The hospital neurologist, who we nicknamed Dr. Doom and Gloom, painted a very scary and dreary picture of how our child would grow up. At only 3 days old, we were bluntly told that a large portion of her brain was dead, she would likely always struggle to walk and use the right side of her body, and they had no idea what her cognitive function would be.

Devastated doesn't even begin to cover it. The first moments of motherhood are already so overwhelming, and this news was almost impossible to process. Thoughts of Why me? Why her? Why us... along with the terrible feeling of thinking it was maybe somehow my fault. That I ate the wrong foods or didn't get enough exercise. Truth be told, I didn't even know babies could have strokes! I had little knowledge of CP and we didn't know any friends or family who had a child with special needs.

With this multitude of conditions, some which we learned at birth and others later on, we were behind on almost all of her milestones. She never crawled and didn't walk until she was about 2 1/2 years old. The amazing thing is, even with all of these setbacks, now at 4 years old, she's able to go up and down our stairs on her own (while holding the railing).

That Saturday, she did the entire staircase without holding onto anything! I was both amazed how much her balance had improved and terrified she would fall, and I wouldn't be fast enough to catch her. My own fear or not though, this is a huge milestone celebration for us! While most parents of mainstream kids might just naturally assume their child will do this, it wasn't even an option which crossed my mind. To say I was on cloud 9, proud parent moment, would be an understatement.

Now comes one of my redeeming qualities. I make a hot breakfast for her almost every day! #ParentingWin

Every Saturday at 10am, my daughter goes to a dance class. As a side note, I was very fortunate to find a dance class that was willing to work with her different abilities and happy to have us in their program. Later in this book is a whole chapter on getting your child into activities and social groups, where I'll share with you how to go about finding a place like this for your child.

This particular Saturday, we actually had a pretty good start to our morning, after recovering from the 4am wakeup. Breakfast goes smoothly instead of the usual pestering her to eat for 2 hours. I get her hair done with only a minimal amount of distress, if you have a daughter you know what I mean here, and we actually manage to leave the house on time! Which is also not usually an easy task.

However, back down the emotional hill; is the short car ride to dance class. We get in the car in a great mood and less

Different Abilities

than 10 minutes later we're getting out of the car with me tossing out empty threats about not going into class and going back home instead. Never a proud parenting moment but I'll sadly admit I am an empty threat-aholoc. One short and very public parking lot argument later, I managed to get my daughter into dance class only a few minutes after its started.

I then had an hour where I don't have to give 100% of my focus to my daughter. I still have to stay in the lobby of the dance studio, so it's not really an hour of free time, but I get to sit with other adults and surf Facebook without interruption, so that's typically a high for me.

As class ends and my daughter and I head to my car, I'm thankful to find, at this moment, she's in a good mood. After dance class is always hit or miss. Sometimes, like today, she is all smiles and actually listens pretty well; while other days are instant meltdowns which leave me feeling humiliated in front of the other parents.

Grateful for the emotional high, I think quickly on my feet about how I can really make the most of this good mood, since I have several more days before my husband comes back into town. We're low on groceries and I know my daughter likes to go to the store, (though she often makes me regret bringing her) so I decide we will stop at the store on the way home.

She's all smiles, even lets me sit her in the cart without a fight, and we actually have a pleasant shopping experience. So much so in fact, when she sees the balloons and asks for one, I decide to reward her good behavior and get it for her. Sadly, just like a real rollercoaster, you can only climb so high before your coaster car glides over the edge and you begin plummeting back toward the earth.

What started as a reward quickly turns into a driving hazard and a game of *laugh and don't listen to mommy*, while I attempt to navigate traffic with a giant balloon floating around my car. Any attempt on my part to get my daughter to keep the balloon out of my line of sight, is rewarded with her kicking my seat, screaming at me, pushing the balloon more into my way, etc. My frustration grows, but as I get the car parked in the garage, we seem to have plateaued a bit.

Inside the house, it's just about 12pm, and I have 2 choices. Try and spend the next 2 hours feeding my daughter lunch and fighting with her about taking a nap, until it actually becomes too late for her to nap at all and we both end up grumpy, or skip lunch & go straight toward the nap. She had a big breakfast only a few hours before, so I decide to try for just the nap. I know it will still be a battle but at least if we start earlier, I might actually win, with enough time to get an hour or so of peace.

To my surprise, getting her up to her room and even out of her dance clothes turns out to be pretty easy! I'm riding high again and in a good mood as I give her a few hugs and kisses and tuck her in for her nap. I knew it was too good to be true though and boy was I right. I'll spare you all the angry and frustrated details but leave you with this. Over an hour later and at one of my lowest points of the day, she's finally asleep at 1:30pm and I get to celebrate by eating my lunch in peace! Truth be told she's really outgrowing naps at this point, but I'll admit to selfishly not being ready myself to let her give up nap time.

Different Abilities

I let her nap for about 2 hours, and I use the time to clean up around the house, organize, get some work and laundry done, you know... mom chores. I wake her up at 3:30pm to find her in a surprisingly good mood and decide on the spot to see if she wants to go to the park for an hour. I don't take her to park often, as we live in a place where most of the year it's too hot to really go out and enjoy it. I also don't personally love the outdoors but that makes me feel like bad mom, so I'm really trying to make more of an effort to let her get out and play. Now that winter is here, it's under 70 and the perfect weather to spend an hour or so outside.

She's thrilled by this idea and getting ready to go proves to not only be easy, but also a low stress activity. I want to drive to the park (it's about a 15-minute walk since her CP means she can't walk very fast) but she insists on walking and I cave with her promise to behave and listen. High again we have a fun time at the park, where I push her in a swing for an hour, but even while I'm having fun, I'm also having an internal mental battle.

My 4-year-old is in the baby swing at the park. You know, the one that has leg holes and a full torso surround, so you can put a baby in there and they won't fall out as you push them. It's not safe for my daughter to swing on the older, flat black swings, as there is nothing to keep her from falling and she can't hold on well on her right side. This leaves the only swing option, as the baby swing. We're lucky in a sense that she's a very small 4-year-old and actually still fits in the baby swing, or I'm quite certain I would be describing a meltdown right now.

At first, we're the only family at the park and I'm having fun just basking in my daughter's happiness as I push her swing. I mentioned it was really nice out though, so as you would expect, other families begin to show up at the park as well. Most of these families have kids around my daughters age and before too long, I am back to feeling low. This time though it's not because of the dynamics between my daughter and me.

I know we're not supposed to compare our child to someone else, but no matter how hard I try not to, I still do it. I see a kid my daughter's age or even younger who can ride a tricycle (my daughter can't) or who can climb a jungle gym (mine can't do that either) or swing in a standard swing, and I mentally plummet back into a low spot. This time it's not because of an argument or frustration, it's envy.

I envy these parents who don't have to wonder if their child will ever be able to do these things. These parents have 100% confidence their child will. To them, it's a natural progression of their child's life. But not for us. As amazing, strong willed, and determined my daughter is, and as much as I try to never put a boundary on her and assume she can't do something; the truth is she may never actually be able to climb a jungle gym or go across the monkey bars.

It's trivial really, because these types of actives don't determine who she will be at all. It's just some kids having fun. I know one million percent that I am SO blessed to have her in my life. My daughter is by far the best thing that has ever happened to me. She's made me a better person in so many ways, I could never list them all. She's smart, determined, and beautiful. She radiates happiness and at only 4 years old she has a deeper understanding of love than most adults.

Different Abilities

I am so grateful to have her in my life and as you're reading this, I don't want you to mistake my envy in moments, for anything other than the fact that I am human. I don't need or want any pity, in fact, most of the time I'm the lucky the one! But the irrational part of us, always thinks the grass is greener on the other side.

In the end, we had our fun at the park and make it back home with a minimal amount of coercion. We had a relatively pleasant dinner together and even hang out on the couch before it's time to get ready for bed. Our bedtime routine is a rollercoaster all on its own, probably much like yours is, but we manage to fit in a little cuddle time before I actually get her into her own bed. A few more ups and downs, hugs and kisses, and by about 8:15pm she's asleep.

My work for the day isn't over. There's still laundry to fold, dishes to wash and more of this book to write, all before I turn into bed myself, around 10pm. I know I'm not alone. I'm not the only mom of a child with special needs or even mainstream, that feels this way; though I do think, when parenting a child with special needs, our rollercoaster tends to have a few more twists and turns than the rides other parents might be on. In the end though, we're all on the ride. Sometimes we're at the top of our game and other times we feel like total failures.

I guess the whole point I'm trying to make is... we're not alone and we don't have to be perfect. Tomorrow is a new day and all any of us can do is try to climb just a little higher.

As you get ready to actually dive into this book now, I wanted to give you an idea of what lies ahead. First and foremost, I am not a *professional*. I'm not a Doctor or a

Therapist, and I have a Bachelors degree in Theatre Arts, not Childhood Development or the like. I am however, a mom of a child with special needs. There are plenty of books from professionals and I'm sure you get daily advice from your child's Dr.'s, Therapist, etc. but sometimes it's really good to have the perspective of another mom.

I've always had a unique way of seeing the world and of solving problems, and I've done just that with my daughter. You might wonder what a mom of a child, who is just over 4 years old, could possibly offer in the way of help, to a parent with a 10-year-old or even a teenager. Maybe you're thinking this book can only help those whose children have CP like my daughter, or only parents who have a single child; but before you stop reading, I promise you that this book does have help to offer you. No matter the age of your child, how many children you have or what their diagnosis is.

I've helped countless moms whose children are all ages and have all sorts of different abilities. I run a private group just for moms like us, that today has over 2,100 members and grows by about 200-300 members a week. These moms have children with all different abilities; including ASD, Down Syndrome, Physical and Mental conditions, CP, etc., and the one thing I hear over and over again is how grateful they are for all the help I've given them. I get daily messages about how they never thought to try something the way I suggested it and it turns out to be the lightbulb moment they've been waiting for.

So, what I mean to say here is this. I'm not an expert and my learning journey is far from complete. This book won't have all the answers, but I can promise you with 100% certainty, you will be grateful you read it. I promise you at some

Different Abilities

moment or another, you will be able to learn from me (likely a lot of moments), laugh with me (or at me which is ok too), and together we can ride this emotional rollercoaster of special needs parenting together.

Chantelle Turner

Different Abilities

Section 1: Self Care

Chapter 1
Sleep

Before even starting to write this book, I interviewed over 150 different moms, who all have children with different special needs. One of the biggest things these parents told me was they need help with sleep. Now, there are a lot of variables when it comes to sleep, so I'm going to cover a few different things.

First, how well you are sleeping can be affected by a bunch of different things, right? The quality of the sleep you get, for most of us moms, probably has a lot to do with our kids. If our kids aren't sleeping, how are we going to sleep? This is something I really want to touch on because as I mentioned in the introduction, it's something that I've been working on with my four year old as well.

My daughter does not sleep through the night very often. She's getting better, but she doesn't sleep all the way through the night most nights. I already told you about the bad habit I started of bringing her into our bed, and if you haven't started that habit yourself yet, I don't encourage giving it a try. I know after countless nights, being woken up several times, the temptation to just have your child sleep with, you can outweigh any potential consequences a more rested you would not risk.

One way we are working on correcting this, happens when I put her to bed. I tell her, if you wake up and it's not morning yet, you need to go back to sleep on your own. I tell her this every night and I have her say it back to me, so I know she was listening and heard what I said. She says, "If I wake up, I'll go back to sleep." Now, does she do that every time? Of course not! This is real life after-all, not a fantasy or movie. With consistent repetition, she's getting better though.

Anything you do with your child is going to take work and repetition, along with positive reinforcement. I always make sure to go way overboard with excitement and praise when she's managed to sleep through the night. We talk about it in the morning, how proud I am of her that she stayed in bed all night and didn't wake up mommy. I smile big and give lots of hugs, letting her know in my voice and body, how truly pleased I am with her! Now, while not all children are as heavily motivated by praise as my daughter, most children do want to please their parents (whether it's on the surface or deeper down inside).

Challenges like potty training or illness can pop up and interrupt your child's ability to stay in bed, even if they want to. At the time of my writing this book, my daughter is in fact working on potty training. It's been about a year long process and she's done really well with not wetting the bed, but she's now waking up at about four o'clock in the morning because she has to go potty. This is good, she's getting up to use the potty! The challenge is, she's not going back to sleep afterward. Once she's used the potty, she's wide awake.

As you can imagine, I don't want to be up at four o'clock in the morning. With my goal of having her let me sleep until 6am, I've been working on ways to get her to have some quiet activities she can do that are safe, but she can do while I'm sleeping. You may be able to get your child to play quietly in their room or even quietly in your room, if that works better for you both. If you allow electronics like an iPad, you may let them watch it as a reward for letting you sleep. Books can also be a good quiet activity but may not hold your child's attention very long. The point here is for you to come up with some prearranged activities that will work for you and them. You may even have to test out several things over the course of a few mornings until you find a good fit.

As a reminder, make sure that your child can do this activity safely on their own, especially if you're asleep. You don't want them to accidentally swallow something or get hurt while you're not awake to watch them. Coloring can also be a great activity, as long as they are well trained about coloring only on paper and such. The big key here is I don't want you to think that you have to force your child to try and go back to sleep. If they're wide awake, trying to force them back to sleep is not going to help or work, and it's likely just going frustrate you.

In some cases, getting your child to stay in their room and in their bed (especially if it's nowhere near morning time) is going to be a better option. This will vary in levels of difficulty based on things like the age and comprehension level of your child, the time of night, how firm you are about them staying in bed, etc. I tell my daughter, if you're not ready to sleep, that's okay but you need to stay in bed. When they're lying in bed, quiet, and resting, they will likely fall back to sleep. It takes work and positive encouragement, but all of these little things come together to help you and your child have a better night sleep.

Once I do wake up, I always thank her for letting me sleep in. I give her positive reinforcement for being quiet, for being good, all those kinds of things. It takes work. It's not perfect every time. Some nights I don't get to go back to sleep. But more often than not, I do!

So, what else can affect our sleep? Maybe your child IS sleeping through the night, but you're not, right? Either you're having a hard time going to sleep yourself or you're waking up throughout the night but you're unsure why. While there can be many causes for this, our diets can drastically affect the quality of our sleep. If you're not giving yourself a healthy diet (and this is true for your child as well) then both of you are going to struggle to sleep well, and through the night. If your stomach is upset, your digestive system's upset, that's likely going to keep you up.

Shutting down our phones and not looking at them before we go to bed, can also help you get a better night sleep. I'm guilty of surfing Facebook while I lay in bed and this can keep me up for an extra 30 minutes to an hour or more! I've often ended up only putting my phone down when I am literally too tired to keep my eyes open. This might seem like a good way to help you fall asleep, but it's not. Looking at a bright phone while in a dark room is not good for your eyes to start. Additionally, it keeps your brain active and sends a confusing message to your body about bedtime and sleep. Later in this book, I'll be covering bedtime routines for your children, but the same overlaying principal applies to us adults too.

We all have some kind of routine we go through each night before bed. Whether you are conscious of it or not, our bodies rely on this routine as a message that it's time to shut down and go to sleep. Things like putting on pajamas, brushing our teeth, etc., that we do every night, send a signal to our brain that our day is over, and we need to sleep. Now that you know, you can see how we might be sending some pretty mixed messages to our bodies if we first go through the bedtime routine, lay down in bed as if we are wanting to go sleep, only to actually pick up our phone or turn on the TV and reengage our brain.

When it's time to go to bed, put your phone down or turn off the TV. Get in bed and let your body relax on its own and go to sleep. Just like our children, this probably won't work instantly the first night you try it. You will likely need to lay in bed awake for a while, for several nights, until your body can actually trust that you really do want to go to sleep. In the end though, this is so much healthier. Turn off the TV and other distractions.

There are also some great products on the market that can help you, if you feel you might need some sleep assistance. I don't recommend giving a bunch of stuff to your child, depending on the age. That's something you should certainly discuss with your doctor, and I'm not recommending any kind of prescription pills, or anything like that. There are however some great natural things that can help you and your child sleep.

Something as simple as essential oils or certain vitamins and minerals, can actually help you fall asleep more naturally and stay asleep throughout the night. When it comes to a more holistic approach to both falling asleep and staying asleep, it's unlikely the first thing you try will work right away. It may end up being a combination of things that finally works for you and your child or it may take you trying out several things, before finding what works. It's also not likely going to be an instant change. It can take several weeks for our bodies to adapt to new sleep habits or get healthy enough to improve how we sleep. Be patient and don't give up.

Personally, I like to use oils like lavender, peppermint, and cedar, in both our bedroom and our daughter's. We have a diffuser that disperses them throughout the room as we sleep at night. The lavender is calming and relaxing, while the peppermint and cedar help to keep our airways open, so we have good breathing as we sleep. There are lots of different essential oils and combinations you can try until you find what works best for you. If you can find a professional naturopath, that is probably one of the best places to start, but you can also do some oil research on you own. Just be sure that you are finding credible sites and not ones who care more about selling you their brand of oils more than reliable facts.

When it comes to vitamins and minerals, there are a lot of options that can help you sleep but it's always best to check with your Dr. before starting something new. Especially if you take any other medications, so you can avoid any potential medication conflicts. Melatonin can be a good supplement and is widely used but be careful with how you use it. Melatonin is something our bodes naturally produce as we get ready to fall asleep. While supplementing it can help you fall asleep, doing so all the time can run the risk of telling your body it no longer needs to produce it on its own.

Non-Caffeinated teas like Chamomile Tea can also be a healthy way to help your body get ready for sleep, though you run the risk of needing to use the restroom more often in the night, which would then interrupt your sleep pattern.

I personally use a supplement called Rest. While I sleep well most nights on my own, I find that when traveling, especially if there is a big change in time zones, my body needs some help. Rest is a sublingual gel you take just before bed and is a combination of vitamins and minerals. I like that helps me fall asleep quickly but does not leave me feeling groggy in the morning like many other options do. If you're interested in learning more about Rest, I'll provide a resource link in the appendix of this book.

Finally, stretching or exercising before bed can be a great way to get your body to relax and will usually help you sleep better overall. You don't need to run a 5K or burn 1,000 calories either. Often times just 5-10 minutes of some simple floor exercise is all you really need. You can find some great bedtime exercise on Youtube and give them a try. Additionally, as you get your body ready for bed this way, you may want to add in some meditation to help your mind relax as well.

As you continue to read this book and especially the remainder of this section on *Self Help*, you will come across other things you can do for yourself, that will tie back to what I have written here and help your sleep. Coming up in this section are chapters on diet, routines, and managing stress, which can all lead back to a healthy night sleep.

Chantelle Turner

www.ingramcontent.com/pod-product-compliance
Lightning Source LLC
LaVergne TN
LVHW051518070426
835507LV00023B/3179